T0065165

Why Is Satan Against Christians?

Paul Antwi

authorHOUSE®

AuthorHouse™
1663 Liberty Drive
Bloomington, IN 47403
www.authorhouse.com
Phone: 833-262-8899

Published by AuthorHouse 12/17/2022

ISBN: 978-1-6655-7881-3 (sc)
ISBN: 978-1-6655-7880-6 (e)

Print information available on the last page.

This book is printed on acid-free paper.

CONTENTS

DEDICATION

This book is dedicated to God the Father and the Lord Jesus Christ who has given me this special gift, and to the Holy Spirit who enables me to study and understand the difficult passages in the Bible and bring it out clearly in a way that everybody benefits. I'm very much grateful to Him.

ACKNOWLEDGEMENT

I am grateful to God the Father, the Son and the Holy Spirit, for granting me this special gift, knowledge and revelations, and enables me study difficult passages in the Bible and bring them out in a way that everyone understands.

Special thanks also go to my dear wife, Wynona Antwi, General Executive Council members of Glorious Mount Zion Teaching And Prayer Ministry International, all church's members in USA, Spain and all branches in Ghana.

I am also very grateful to Rev. Saka Ntiamoah of the church of Pentecost USA who wrote the foreword in very delightful notice. The Editors Rev. Godwin Ampofo and Mrs. Gifty Ampofo-The church of Pentecost USA, and anyone who has helped me in anyway to make this book come out again successfully.

God Richly Bless You all!

FOREWORD

In any given battle, the greatest weapon to wield against the enemy is a true knowledge of the strength and weakness of that enemy.

The Bible makes it clear that we are not ignorant about the schemes of the devil. With solid knowledge of the schemes of the enemy of your soul, you can defeat him.

It is precisely this vital understanding that the author, a man whose character matches with his action offers in this book-WHY IS SATAN AGAINST CHRISTIANS? This is a book with an in-depth exploration of the reason why Satan attacks you.

By reading this book you can understand how to exploit the weakness of the enemy and use the biblical solutions offered to defend yourself against Satan.

The author **indeed offers a blue print** for you, to understand and overcome the trials and temptations that almost all believers face in their lives.

This book will inspire you to take a new look at your life through this excellent exposure of Satan's strategies and the solution offered will cause a fresh faith to arise and awareness will be created to face the enemy head on.

Why Is Satan Attack Christians; is a book of hope and victory, and I encourage any honest person wishing to live a more fruitful and victorious life should read it.

Reverend Saka Ntiamoah
Houston District Pastor
The church of Pentecost, U.S.A. INC.

INTRODUCTION

"Be self-controlled and alert. Your enemy the devil prowls around like a roaming lion looking for someone to devour". 1Peter 5:8. ***"For they (devils) cannot sleep till they do evil, they are robbed of slumber till they make someone fall". Prov.4:16.***

The above two passages indicate that, Satan and his accomplices chase Christians everyday to make them fall. The question this book is asking is why are they always against us? Why do they try to make us fall, or cause others to do the evil things which they are to separate themselves from? These are some of the questions believers want answers to. We thank God that this book provides answers to all these questions and helps believers to know and combat the hold Satan may have in their lives.

This book is therefore recommended to all Christians so that they may know what is expected of them and not to fall prey to Satan and his accomplices. Again this book reveals the Lord's will concerning faithful worship without any fear of evil. But to know what the Lord's Will is, in order to worship Him faithfully without any fear of evil. (Eph.5:17, Prov.1:33). Finally this book will appeal to all readers and also remain beneficial to especially those who desire salvation.

All the scriptures were taken from NIV/TNIV unless otherwise stated. However, some statements in these versions seem to be incorrect but in order not to complicate it, I want the editors to maintain it. So if any statement quoted directly from any Bible Version in this book is confusing, please refer to KJV or any Bible of your choice for better understanding.

CHAPTER 1

SATAN IS THE RULER OF THE WORLD

Satan was once a leading angel of God called Lucifer. Due to his pride and subsequent rebellion against the Almighty God, whose kingdom cannot be shaken nor overthrown (Heb.12:28-29), he was cast down to the earth where he is known as Satan—the devil.

"How art thou fallen from heaven, O Lucifer, son of the morning, how art thou cast down to the ground, which didst weaken the nation. For thou said in thy heart I will ascend into heaven. I will exalt my throne above the stars of God. I will sit also upon the mount of the congregation in the side of the north. I will ascend above the heights of the clouds. I will be like the Most High. Yet thou shall be brought down to the side of the pit". Isaiah 14:12-15. (KJV)

The above scripture clearly explains that in spite of the evil plans of Satan, the Almighty God was able to cast him and his followers down, because the kingdom of God cannot be shaken. The coup to overthrow the kingdom of God could not succeed, but he won a third (1/3) of the angels, who have become the "evil spirits". (Rev.12:4)

When Satan was cast down to the earth, he lost the beauty and the glory of God he had once possessed. (Ezek.28:11-17). Unfortunately, Satan's evil ambition did not change and consequently, he devised another plan to take God's Throne on this earth. Since he lost his position with God, he has become an enemy to God, opposing whatever God does, including the man God created to take care of the earth. God gave Adam authority over the earth and told him to keep it under his dominion. Regrettably, he listened to his wife—Eve, disobeying God and ate from the tree God commanded them not to eat from. (See Gen.3:1-7).

Satan was able to deceive Eve, the woman God created to help Adam. He convinced her that the tree of knowledge of good and evil which God had commanded them not to eat from was not really bad. Rather, he lured her into believing that eating from this tree would make them like God. At that juncture, Madam Eve who was delighted to be like God, trusted the devil who is a liar because he is the father of all lies, (See John 8:44) and she ate the fruit from the tree. Unfortunately Mr. Adam also joined her and ate the fruit although he knew it was a lie. (See Gen.2:9, 15-24, 3:1-6, 1Tim.2:14). Through that one act of sin, man lost the glory of God and the dominion over all creations (See Gen.3:7-24). Satan then took over the throne vacated by man and exercised his authority over it; he then became the ruler of the earth (See John 14:30, 1John 5:19).

Since then, sin and death filled the earth bestowing unto all generations that followed Adam and Eve an inheritance of the fallen human nature. Hence, bringing all under the power and dominion of Satan (See Rom.5:12, Heb.2:14-15, Eph.2:1-3, Rom.3:23). Man's assigned dominion over all creation would have been perpetual had man obeyed God. (Gen.2:9, 15-17, Heb.2:5-8).

Truly God did not give up on man because of his sins, instead He set into motion another great plan; the plan to save mankind from Satan's power and restore him to His original state of being His son and sharing His Throne. He prepared the coming of the Savior Jesus Christ for the world to save mankind from Satan's power. "**For as in Adam all die, so in Christ all will be made alive". 1Cor.15:22.** The Prophet Isaiah saw this great plan and prophesied about it (See Isaiah 9:6-7). Evidently, God's perfect plan worked out nicely at the right time through Jesus Christ. "**When the time had fully come, God sent His Son, born of a woman, born under the law to redeem those under law, that we might receive the full right of sons". Gal.4:4-5. (Matt.1:18-25, John 1:12-13)**

However, when one accepts Christ Jesus and becomes born again, Satan has no authority over him. That person has crossed over from death unto life and has received the glory and fellowship of God which was lost through Adam in the Garden of Eden.

Although the death of Jesus Christ took believers away from Satan's power, it did not take away Satan's power to control the world. Since the fall of man, Satan has been the ruler of the world, therefore if anyone is in this world without accepting Jesus Christ as his Lord and personal savior, he is under the devil's bondage, he is dead, doomed, depraved, and naturally an object of God's wrath. (See Eph.2:1-13). The moment he accepts Jesus Christ as Lord and personal savior, God saves him by His grace and mercy. **"As for you, you were DEAD in your TRANSGRESSION AND SIN, in which you used to live when you followed the ways of this world and the RULER of the kingdom of the air, the spirit who is now at work in those who are DISOBEDIENT. All of us also lived among them at one time, gratifying the cravings of our nature and following its desire and thought. Like the rest, we were by nature OBJECTS OF WRATH. But because of His great love for us, God who is rich in mercy, made us alive with Christ even when we were dead in transgression. It is by grace you have been saved. And God raised us up with Christ Jesus and seated us with Him in heavenly realms in Christ Jesus". Eph.2:1-**6.

Dear readers, this is what God has done for mankind through Jesus Christ which has inspired the Apostle Paul's declaration that; "**If someone is in Christ, he is a new creation, THE OLD HAS GONE, THE NEW HAS COME" 2Cor.5:17**. The old that was doomed, dead, depraved and under Satan's authority is gone, and the new that qualifies us automatically as Sons of God has come. In this case, Satan has no authority over your life (See 1John 5:18-19). For this very reason, he is trying all means possible to win you back to his camp so that your salvation bought with the precious blood of our Lord Jesus Christ can be lost. (See 1Peter 1:17-21). Satan and his "evil spirits" have been condemned, so they are working hard to have more souls with them in their rebellion and condemnation.

Believers, this is the secret behind why they (devils) do not sleep at all until they have caused someone to fall, thereby subsequently populating their rebellious empire. Therefore be on your guard (Mark 13:23). This explains why believers are being chased in every way possible such as in their marriages, finances, health etc. If you are always being chased by the devil, try to stand firm, never lose heart nor deny your faith in Christ for the painful trial you are going through. In all this, keep pressing on toward the goal aiming at winning the prize for which Christ has called you heavenward in Christ Jesus (See Phil.3:10-14, 1Peter 1:6-7, 4:12-16, 5:10, Rom.8:17-18, Phil.1:27-30).

Dear reader, I am convinced this chapter has answered one of the questions bothering the minds of believers, and has revealed the reason why Satan and his accomplices are always very busy attacking believers. The title of this book is a question; **"WHY IS SATAN AGAINST CHRISTIANS"?** The simple answer is that, since you have been saved by the blood of Jesus from his power and dominion, it means the enemy has lost the battle to repossess you from his enemy-God. For this reason, he has to fight aggressively with the objective of winning you into his dominion in order that you may join him in condemnation.

Interestingly you may find life very easy and enjoyable while in the devil's kingdom. However, the minute Christ Jesus appears in the picture, you may face lots of problems such as persecution, unemployment, financial constrains and others (See Psalm 34:19). Since the reasons for these assaults have been revealed to you, the most important thing to do is to hold on fast to your holy faith. This is what the Apostle Paul said when he became an apostle of Christ. **"For it has been granted to you on behalf of Christ, not only to believe on him but also to suffer for Him. Since you are going through the same struggle you saw I had and now hear that I still have" Phil.1:29-30.**

When he was in the world and under the devil's authority, he was free and the "tormentor—in—chief" of those who had accepted Christ Jesus. When he accepted Christ Jesus and became an Apostle, the problems he faced were designed to influence him to deny his faith in God. But he stood firm and said; **"I press on toward the goal to WIN THE PRIZE for which God has called me heavenwards in Christ Jesus". Phil.3:14**.

The next question to be answered in the next chapter is; what can Satan and his "evil spirits" do to believers? Can they harm God's children?

CHAPTER 2

WHAT CAN SATAN AND HIS EVIL SPIRITS DO TO CHRISTIANS?

When someone receives Christ Jesus as his Lord and personal savior and is born again, Satan and his accomplices have no authority over him. The enemy has neither the right to touch him nor his possessions. Although the battle to capture the new believer will still continue, it is very impossible for the devil to succeed. In short, Satan cannot harm the children of the Almighty God in anyway, because our God is strong, the Lord Almighty is His name and He has enough angels to protect His children from the devil and his collaborators (See Jer.50:34, Psalm 91:1-16, Heb.1:14, Exod.23:20, Psalm 34:7). **"We know that anyone born of God does not continue to sin, the One who was born of GOD KEEPS HIM SAFE, AND THE EVIL ONE CANNOT HARM HIM" 1John 5:18. "So we say with confidence, the Lord is my HELPER, I will not be AFRAID, what can human being (or Satan) do to me?" Heb.13:6. "But the Lord is with me like a MIGHTY WARRIOR; so my persecutors will STUMBLE and not prevail. They will FAIL AND BE THOROUGHLY DISGRACED; their dishonor will never be forgotten". Jer.20:11. "What, then, shall we say in response to these things? IF GOD IS FOR US, WHO CAN BE AGAINST US?" Rom.8:31.**

Believers, we can see from the above scriptures that with God on our side, no weapon formed by Satan and his accomplices can work against us in any way. This is what the death of Jesus Christ has done for mankind. Through His death, believers have received the fellowship and glory of

God which protect us from the evil one. Jesus said; "**The prince of this world (referring to Satan) is coming. He has no hold on me". John 14:30**. The meaning of this passage is that; Satan is prowling around like a roaring lion looking for believers who are no more under his dominion to devour, (1Peter 5:8). Since we have accepted Jesus Christ and have become the children of the Almighty God, Satan has no hold on us. Satan cannot harm us in any way, because Jesus Christ paid all our debts on the cross with His precious blood (See 1Peter 1:17-21). If someone is in the Lord, he is a new creation (2Cor.5:17) and therefore has been freed from the bondage of the devil.

Dear reader, if you are already in Christ Jesus, the devil has no hold on you. But for those of you, who have not accepted Jesus Christ as your Lord, you are still under the devil's bondage and he has the power to do whatever he wants to you. Therefore endeavor to be among those who are in Christ Jesus by believing and accepting Jesus Christ as your Lord and personal savior. I want to assure you that Christ came to this earth to save us from sin and the bondage of Satan. **"Here is a trustworthy saying that deserves FULL ACCEPTANCE; Christ Jesus came into the world to save sinners—of whom I am the worst". 1Tim.1:15. (Also see 1 John 3:8)**

When we talk of sinners, it does not only refer to those who are doing evil, but anyone who has not accepted Jesus Christ as his Lord and personal savior is also a sinner irrespective of the life he is leading. A biblical example is Cornelius who was a very **good man** but was not a **righteous man** until when he accepted Jesus into his life as his Lord and personal savior (See Acts 10:1-48). In view of this, anyone who has not as yet accepted Jesus is still a descendant of Adam and qualifies to be labeled as a **SINNER! "For all have sinned and fall short of the glory of God, and are justified freely by his grace through the redemption that came by Christ Jesus. God presented him as a sacrifice of atonement through faith in his blood. He did this to demonstrate his justice because in his forbearance he had left sins committed before hand UNPUNISHED, he did it to demonstrate his justice at the present time, so as to just and the one who justifies those who have faith in Jesus". Rom.3:23-26. "Therefore, just as sin entered the world through one man and death through sin, and in this way death came to all men, because all sinned". Rom.5:12.**

The preceding passages reveal that God is just, and He does things in justice. Although he had given Adam the authority to rule the earth, unfortunately Adam also lost it to Satan. Since this just God did not want to snatch it away from Satan unlawfully, He sent our Lord Jesus Christ to die as a payment for the penalty of our debts (sins).

As you read further, this should be good news to you. The chance is now and the time is right to accept Jesus Christ into your life if you have not already done so. The Bible says "The word is near you, it is in your mouth and in your heart, and this word is the word of faith we are proclaiming. If you confess with your mouth that Jesus is Lord and believe in your heart that God raised him from the dead, you will be saved. For it is with your heart that you believe and are justified and it is your mouth that you confess and are saved". Rom.10:8-10. At this point, if anyone has been touched by the Spirit of God and wants to accept Him now, please feel free and say this short prayer; "**Our Father in heaven, I thank you for the love you have for me, that you sent your Son Jesus Christ to die for my sins. I believe in Him and accept Him as my Lord and personal savior. I ask Him to come into my heart right now. Thank you for hearing me in Jesus' name, Amen".**

If anyone has said this prayer faithfully, he has been born again and has crossed over from death (spiritually) to life, and all his sins have been forgiven and washed away by the precious blood of our Lord Jesus Christ. Jesus is now your Lord and savior. Satan has no hold on you. You cannot be touched nor be harmed, because your redeemer is strong, and the Lord Almighty is His name (See Jer.50:34). The enemy is well aware of the principle that it is impossible for them to harm the children of God Almighty. "**We know that anyone born of God does not continue to sin; the one who was born of God KEEPS HIM SAFE, AND THE EVIL ONE CANNOT HARM HIM". 1John5:18.**

From this lesson, we realize that Satan is still controlling the world, but he and his accomplices cannot touch nor harm those who are in Christ Jesus. Again it is important for those who have Christ to stay in His kindness in order for God to keep them safe. Sometime past, when they (devils) attacked someone seriously and brutally and when Jesus got there to save him, the enemy said **"What do you want with us, Son of God? They shouted. Have you come here to torture us before the appointed time?"**

Matt.8:29. What happened here shows us that Satan can do whatever he likes to those who are not in Christ Jesus. Thanks be to God that Jesus was able to save him from the devil's hands—that was His mission on the earth. "**The reason why the Son of God appeared was to DESTROY THE DEVIL'S WORKS". 1John 3:8.**

Believers! These evil spirits were begging Jesus not to destroy them—which means Jesus could have destroyed them, but chose not to kill, bomb nor whip them. He just destroyed their business of attacking that person. In fact, I wonder how some believers are able to **WHIP AND STONE** Satan and his accomplices. Which way? They are in control of the whole world as rulers and our Lord Jesus Christ is aware of this, because the time set to destroy them has yet not come—that is what they asked Jesus. Until the time set to destroy them comes, whether we like it or not, whether we accept it or not, they will still be controlling the world. Again, they have the authority to attack and harm those who are under their control. Those who are in Christ Jesus, they have no hold on them. (See Jer.20:11, John 14:30, 1John 5:18-21, 3:8, Heb.13:6)

From this lesson, believers should stop attributing all their problems and sufferings to Satan. **Satan and his accomplices have no power over the children of Almighty God**!!!

CHAPTER 3

THEY CAUSE AND DECEIVE BELIEVERS TO SIN

We have learnt that Satan and his accomplices have no power over the children of God (Christians). For this reason, we should not recognize them in our problems and sufferings. Now if they are not responsible for our problems, then why are they chasing us all the time? What are their chances in the lives of believers? What can they do to us if they prevail against us? The answer to these questions have been provided as the heading for this chapter; **"THEY DECEIVE AND CAUSE BELIEVERS TO SIN".**

When Adam fell and lost his position through disobedience, Satan realized that God hates sin and does not want His children to keep on sinning, after having known the truth. (See Heb.10:26-31, 6:4-6) **He knows this is the only way to get God's people to his dominion,** thus all that he does to God's people is to **ENTICE OR LURE** them to disobey God's word and keep on sinning. The Apostle Paul taught believers about the deceitful schemes of the devil. (Eph.4:14, 2Cor.2:11) When Adam sinned, Satan did not do anything to him again, all that he wanted from him is what he did—DISOBEYED GOD. When a believer disobeys God, it is God's prerogative to discipline him. **Fortunately for the devil, this disciplinary action of God helps him to get these disobedient believers into his dominion.**

Now, how did Satan know to use disobedience to separate believers from God's love? He himself fell from his position with God by just planning to do something wrong. In fact, he did not even do it, but the fact that he was planning to do so was known to the Omniscient, Omnipresent and Omnipotent God, resulted in his expulsion from his place forever. God did not give him a second chance to repent. (See Isaiah 14:12-15). From that time, he always tries to throw a challenge at God and accuse Him of unjustly casting him down from his position. That is why God penalized Adam and Eve and expelled them from the Garden of Eden. In fact, there was nobody at that time apart from Adam and his wife, but in order for Satan not to blame God of injustice, God drove them out and used cherubim to replace them. (See Gen.3:1-24) Since then, Satan habitually accuses anyone who commits any offence hoping that God will punish them. Let's consider this passage; "**Then he showed me Joshua, the high priest standing before the angel of the Lord, and Satan STANDING AT HIS RIGHT SIDE TO ACCUSE HIM. The Lord said to Satan, the Lord rebukes you Satan! The Lord who has chosen Jerusalem rebukes you! Now Joshua was dressed in FILTHY CLOTHES as he stood before the angel. The angel said to those who were standing before him, 'Take off his FILTHY CLOTHES'. Then he said to Joshua, 'See, I have taken away your SIN, and I will put fine garments on you". Zachariah 3:1-4. (Zach.3:1-10).**

When you read this scripture from verse one to ten you will understand the point I have raised. According to the passage, Satan was accusing Joshua that he had sinned or had been clothed in sin, and for that matter, he was expecting God to judge or punish him and not give him a second chance to repent. But the Lord stood firm this time and ignored Satan's accusation—implying that the offence Joshua had committed could be forgiven. (See Psalm 32:1-2, Isaiah 43:25, 1John 5:16-17) This is to tell us that all sins are not equal as some believers presume. In fact, this point has been clearly explained in my second book which will soon arrive at the market after this publication.

Satan and his accomplices work relentlessly to lure or cause believers to sin. **"For they (devils) sleep not, except they have done mischief, and their SLEEP IS TAKEN AWAY, UNLESS THEY CAUSE SOMEONE TO FALL". Prov.4:16.** According to this passage, if any of the evil spirits tries to sleep without causing any believer to sin, that spirit has a big case to answer before his master Satan. Their duty is to cause believers to sin! When any of them succeeds in causing a believer to sin, their master Satan uses it as a basis for accusation and demands a possible disciplinary action from God with the hope of getting those believers under his control. **(See Jer.30:11-15, Heb.12:4-11, 2Sam.7:14)** But some of these believers caught in sin perceive God's punishment for their sins as too harsh and Satan therefore capitalizes on that feeling. If that sinful believer does not accept the disciplinary measures in good faith and tries to run away from God's presence, then, Satan gets him, steals his mind from God and this believer in turn regards God as unfaithful in His promises. "**The thief comes only to steal, kill and destroy". John 10:10.**

Believers should do well to be afraid of sin instead of Satan. They should run away from sin just like Joseph ran away and left his shirt in the hands of Potiphar's wife and saved his position in the Lord. (See Gen.39:1-23) So long as the believer has not sinned, no matter what problem he encounters, he will come out victorious. Therefore, believers should be advised to stay in the discipline of God and accept it in good faith. Consider this passage; "**And you have forgotten the word of encouragement that addresses you as sons; my son, do not make light of the Lord's discipline, and do not lose heart when He rebukes you because the Lord disciplines those He loves, and He punishes everyone He accepts as sons".** Heb.12:5-6.

When a believer is being disciplined by God, and faces some problems, he may think it is Satan who is causing him those problems. Therefore, instead of repenting and praying for forgiveness, he rather attends to prayer camps and turns to other sources to be delivered, but this has nothing to do with deliverance, because nobody can deliver a person from God's hands. "**It is a dreadful thing to fall into the hands of the living God". Heb.10:31 "Yet they rebelled and grieved His Holy Spirit, so He (God) Himself TURNED AND BECAME THEIR ENEMY AND FOUGHT AGAINST THEM". Isaiah 63:10. "I am with you and will save you, declares the Lord. Though I completely destroy all the nations among which I scatter you, I WILL NOT COMPLETELY DESTROY YOU. I WILL DISCIPLINE YOU BUT ONLY WITH JUSTICE; I WILL NOT LET YOU GO ENTIRELY UNPUNISHED. I have struck you as enemy would and punished you as would the cruel, because of your**

guilt which is so great and your sins so many. Why do you cry out over your wounds, your pains that have no cure? Because of your great guilt and many sins, I have done these things to you". Jer.30:11-15. "To deny a man his right before the Most High, to deprive a man of justice-would not the Lord see such things? Who can speak and have it happen if the Lord had not DECREED it? Is it not from the mouth of the Most High that both CALAMITIES AND GOOD THINGS come from? Why should any living man complain when punished for his sins?" Lam.3:33-39. "The Lord brings death and make alive; He brings down to the grave and He raises up. The Lord sends POVERTY AND WEALTH; He humbles and He exalts. He raises the poor from the dust and lifts the need from the ash heap. He seats them with princes and has them inherit a throne of honor. It is not by strength that one prevails". 1Sam.2:6-9.

All these passages clearly show us that our heavenly Father may be responsible for our predicaments and sufferings due to our disobedience and many sins. Lamentations chapter three explains this clearly to us; verse 35 says, 'if someone denies you of your right or cheats you, understand it is God who allows him to do that to you, to discipline you of the sin you have committed which should have been avoided'. God uses many different ways to discipline His children for their wrong deeds. Sometimes, some believers can not stand firm in the discipline of God because of how it is inflicted unexpectedly. God can use your church member, a deacon, deaconess, an elder, a pastor or your own family member, even your loving spouse can be used to show you a great lesson in life. Your father, mother, brother, sister, uncle or a very close friend can be used to discipline you if you commit any offence which demands discipline because God says, He will not let none of His guilty children go ENTIRELY UNPUNISHED. (See Jer.30:11, Isaiah 63:10). Sometimes, He uses a very wicked person to discipline these erring believers. **"I will be his father, and he will be my son. WHEN HE DOES WRONG, I WILL PUNISH HIM WITH A ROD WIELDED BY HUMAN BEINGS, WITH FLOGGINGS INFLICTED BY HUMAN HANDS. But my love will never be taken away from him, as I took it away from Saul, whom I removed from before you". 2 Sam.7:14-15.**

One thing I want to remind believers is that, no matter how God's discipline is, He will not leave you in the hands of the devil, this gives us hope that if we endure, we will receive the promise. *"BUT MY LOVE WILL NEVER BE TAKEN AWAY FROM HIM". 2 Samuel 7:15. "But Zion said, 'The Lord has FORSAKEN me, the Lord has FORGOTTEN me'. Can a mother forget the baby at her breast and have no compassion for the child she has borne? Though she may forget, I will not forget you!* ***See I have engraved you on the palms of my hands****, your walls are ever before". Isaiah 49:14-17.* I hope this passage will help believers to know now where they have been **ENGRAVED**—in the palms of God's hands, which is impossible for the devil to torment you without God's approval.

The book of Lamentations 3:37 asks an important question that; "*Who can speak and have it happen if the Lord had not decreed it?"* In this case, someone may curse you, but if God does not approve, it will not work. Verse 38 says*; both good and calamity are from God's mouth.* To explain this briefly, our loving Father in heaven is aware of whatever happens to us, whether good or bad (calamity), for a reason best known to only Him. Satan and his accomplices have no part to play, but causing you to rebel (sin) against God is their duties.

When the Bible says the devil prowls like the roaring lion looking for someone to devour, it means they (devil and his accomplices) are looking for believers to cause or entice them to sin against God. The devil knows very well that if a believer commits a sin, stays in it and keeps on sinning, God will not let him go ENTIRELY UNPUNISHED, (see Jer.30:11, 2 Sam.7:14-15) so he relies on these punishments and disciplines to take advantage of those erring believers. *When a believer is being disciplined by God, the devil lets him know that God is so wicked to His children. This is where some of them start questioning the existence of God.* When the devil visited Eve in the Garden of Eden, he was able to convince her that God is so wicked for not wanting to let them know the truth, and she disobeyed God and instead obeyed Satan (See Gen.3:1-8).

Now let us consider that incidence; why did the devil not kill or hurt Eve? He had an opportunity to kill her and Adam because God was not physically with them at that time. Why did the devil not make any attempt to kill them? This is to tell some of you who are afraid of the devil that he has no right to touch the children of the Almighty God. (See 1 John 5:18-21, Jer.20:11, Rom.8:31, Heb.13:6)

So far, I hope believers have now seen the duties of the devil and his accomplices.—their duties are to cause, entice or lure believers into sin, because they know the consequence ahead of those erring believers. (See Isaiah 63:10, Jer.30:11-16, Heb.12:4-11, Heb. 6:4-6, 10:26-27, 31)

Lamentations 3:39-44 explains that instead of complaining about your sufferings you must examine your ways and test them, and if you discover that you have committed any offence against God, repent and return to Him. Going around some places to seek help from self acclaimed 'men of God' will help the devil to confuse, deceive and win you over. (See John 10:10, 2 Cor.2:11, 2Thess.2:9-12, 2Cor.11:13-15, 1Tim.5:15, 4:1-2, 2Peter 2:1-10). Therefore, believers should not try to run away from God's discipline, rather, they should co-operate with Him and wait patiently for Him to restore them back to His loving kindness.(Psalm 37:7, Isaiah 26:3)

It is popular for the devil when believers blame him for their trials and retributions. Christians are not dealing with the devil in our retribution and tribulations, but with God. Although Job was attacked by Satan, yet he was not dealing with him but with God. He knew very well that without God's approval, (Lam.3:37-38) the devil had no power to torment him. He said; 'The hand of God has struck me' Job19:21, 13:15. Job refused to acknowledge Satan in any of his trials and tribulations.

It is comforting to know that we have a very big God who is always on our side, when we place ourselves in his hands He is able to save us from all that we fear no matter what the circumstances may seem like. "*What shall we say in response to this? IF GOD IS FOR US, WHO CAN BE AGAINST US?*" Rom.8:31. **"But the Lord is with me like a Mighty Warrior; so my persecutors will stumble and will not prevail, their dishonor will never be forgotten". Jer.20:11. "So we say with confidence, the Lord is my HELPER; I will not be AFRAID; what can man (uses by Satan) do to me?" Heb.13:6.**

Frankly, Satan and God's reaction to believers in general is just like the case of the snake and the frog. The story goes like this; the Snake claimed to be the most poisonous animal, while the frog also challenged that it was more poisonous than the snake, but the snake was highly feared by people. Consequently, both of them agreed to hide in a place and bite an individual and see whose sting can kill him. The snake accepted to bite first and when it bit the person it quickly disappeared and the frog appeared immediately. The person was about to cry for help that he had been bitten by a snake, but as soon as he saw the frog he said "oh, it's just a frog", so he did not take it seriously and did not die. When it came to the turn of the frog, it bit the person and disappeared and the snake immediately appeared, when the person saw the snake, he screamed for help that he had been bitten by a snake. When people came to his aid and wanted to rush him to the hospital, he died on the spot! This ended the argument and the snake then accepted that the frog was the most poisonous animal, and asked it to give it some of its poison.

The moral of this story is that both believers and unbelievers know that God is LOVE (GOOD) and Satan is WICKED (BAD). So whenever anything good happens to us, we know it is from God, and all the bad things which come to us are from Satan. Surely, it is God who is in-charge and responsible for the lives of believers, whether good or calamity. Satan is been feared by people, but if believers obey God, He is able to protect us from the devil. Consider these two passages for the proof of the point I have raised; "**See, it is I who CREATED the blacksmith who fans the coals into frame and forges a weapon fit for its work. AND IT IS I WHO HAVE CREATED THE DESTROYER TO WORK HAVOC; no weapon forged against you will prevail, and you will refute every tongue that accuses you. This is the heritage of the servants of the Lord, and this is their vindication from me, declares the Lord." Isaiah 54:16-17. "I form the light and CREATE DARKNESS, I bring prosperity and CREATE DISASTER; I, the LORD, DO ALL THESE THINGS." Isaiah 45:7**. Is there any lesson from these two passages? God is making it clear in this passage that He was the One who created the destroyer to cause troubles to mankind, so He has the power to allow him to destroy and He has the power to stop him from causing havoc. (See 2Sam.24:16). This implies that anything that happens to the believer is first known, allowed or approved by God before it can happen. (See Lam.3:37-38)

I am not trying to put fears in believers about God, but I want to expose the devil's trick to people and believers; "**In order that Satan might not outwit us. For we are not unaware of his schemes". 2Cor. 2:11**. What I am trying to do in this book is to help believers to be afraid of sin but not Satan and his accomplices. Because, the scriptures assure us that the Holy Spirit who lives in us is God, hence we are stronger than the devil and his accomplices. (See John 4:24, Acts 5:3-4) *"You dear children are from God and have overcome them (devils) because the One who is in you is GREATER than the one who is in the world" 1John 4:4. "I write to you, young men, because you have overcome the evil one. I write to you, young men, because you are STRONG and the word of God lives in you and you have OVERCOME the evil one" 1John 2:13-14.*

Does the word of God live in you? If your answer is yes, then, why are you afraid of the devils and blame them of all your predicaments? All you have to do is to accept Jesus Christ into your life, and those who have already accepted Him must be led by the Holy Spirit so that the devil will be conquered under their foot. Any believer who is being tormented by the devil may not really be a Christian—Jesus' disciple, but he is a church-goer! (Professed Christian) Because the scripture makes it clear that Satan has no power over the children of God. **What he and his accomplices can do to Christians is to lure or entice them to disobey their God and if any of them tries to run away from the discipline he may face from the sins he has committed, they take that advantage to steal him, destroy and finally kill him.** (See John 10:10, 1Cor.2:11, Heb.12:4-11) You may read the following texts for more details of the point raised. Lam.3:35-44, 1Sam.2:6-9, 2Sam. 24:10-17, Eccl.5:6, Deut.28:63-66, Jer.20:11-12, 30:11-15, 31:28, Ezek.36:29-32, 2Sam.7:14, Rom. 8:31, Heb.12:4-11, 1Pet.3:10-12, 1John 2:13-14, 4:4, 5:18-21.

Let us look at the lives of the Israelites as the evidence of this lesson. Kindly read the following chapters of Numbers and follow me as I explain them to you, Numbers 22, 23, 24, 25. Read the whole chapters and see how God lives with His people. Chapter 22 talks about Balak, son of Zippor and the king of Moab. The king sent messengers to summon the prophet Balaam, son of Beor, to come and CURSE the Israelites for him so that they could be defeated. Initially, God stopped him when he consulted Him, but allowed him later to go for that assignment. Chapter 23 also explains that instead of cursing them, prophet Balaam rather BLESSED them. King Balak couldn't understand what Balaam was doing, and he asked him, why he rather BLESSED them instead of CURSED them as was the deal? In response the Prophet Balaam replied; *"HOW CAN I CURSE THOSE WHOM THE LORD HAS NOT CURSED? HOW CAN I DENOUNCE THOSE WHOM GOD HAS NOT DENOUNCED*?" Numbers 23:8.

The question in Lamentation 3:37 supports the answer prophet Balaam gave to king Balak; "*Who can speak and have it happen if the Lord had not decreed it?*" So if we consider these two passages, Numbers 23:8 and Lam.3:37, the result is if someone curses you and God does not allow or decree it, it cannot happen to you. If the devil plans to kill you or to cause you any harm and the Lord is on your side, all their efforts will not be successful. (See Rom.8:31, Heb.13:6, Jer.20:11) If they plan to destroy your business, marriage or any other thing, and God does not allow it, it cannot happen to you, because the kingdom of God is not a matter of TALK, but of POWER. (See 1Cor.4:20, 2Cor.10:3-6).

The devil or anybody being used by him cannot curse those who are in Christ Jesus (children of God), nor can they harm nor cause any damage to the people of God, unless God allows it for the reason best known to Him. (Rev.2:10, Jer.20:11-12, 2Sam.7:14, Jer.30:11-15, Heb.13:6, 12:4-11) Therefore, prophet Balaam could not curse the Israelites whom the Lord had blessed for the sake of father Abraham.

However, king Balak did not give up easily and took prophet Balaam to different places, thinking he was not seeing them properly. But all attempts made to curse the Children of God proved futile. Whenever he opened his mouth to pronounce curses, he ended up professing blessings. In dismay, Balak said to Balaam, "*What have you done to me? I brought you to curse my enemies, but you have done nothing but bless them! He answered and said, must I not speak what the Lord puts in my mouth?*" Numbers 23:11-12. **"Then Balak said to Balaam, neither curse them at all nor bless them at all. Balaam answered, Did I not tell you I must do whatever the Lord says?"** Number 23:25-26.

Numbers chapter 24 explains how Balak and Balaam after their quarrel, tried the fourth and final oracles to curse the Israelites, but all the curses turned into blessings because they were the Almighty God's children and no-one can curse them and have it happen. This applies to every Christian who is being led by the Spirit of God. (See John 4:23-24, Rom.8:14, 1John 5:18-21) If we as believers understand this fact, stay away from sin and continue to stay in the kindness of God, whatever the devil and his accomplices will plan against us cannot materialize. (Isaiah 54:17, Rom.11:22).

Now let's find out how king Balak and his people were able to subdue the Israelites after prophet Balaam failed to pronounce curses on them. Numbers chapter 25 explains that when Balak and his people realized that they could not curse the Israelites, they made another plan which really worked for them. They found out that God who was in-charge of the Israelites hates sin, especially adultery, fornication and worshipping of other gods, which is His greatest abomination. So they realized that if they could lure them into these sins which are God's abomination, He Himself will fight them. (Isaiah 63:10)

When the arrangement was completed, the Moabites went into the camp of the Israelites and began to indulge in sexual immorality with them. Again, the Israelites ate and bowed down to the Moabite gods, and they joined them to worship the Baal of Poer. For this reason, the Lord's anger burnt against His own people, fought against them and killed them heavily to confirm the passage read in Isaiah 63:10. It was Phinehas who turned the Lord's anger away from them. But those who died in that plague were numbered twenty-four thousand. The Lord said to Moses, 'Phinehas has turned my ANGER away from the Israelites, for he was zealous as I am for my honor among them, so that is my zeal I did not put an end to them. (See Numbers 25:6-11)

The people who could not be cursed nor harmed by anybody, any nation not even the devil, were killed by their own loving Father who is supposed to have protected them from any danger. Why? Because of their great guilt and many sins.(See Jer.30:11-15) This is clear evidence that the only thing the devil can do to God's children is deceiving or causing them to do evil things in the sight of God so that their Father will discipline them. (See Heb.12:4-11). In this case, if one is being disciplined by his Father in heaven, he should not blame the devil that he is causing some problems to him.

The diagram below shows how God lives with His people (Christians)

(1)The Kindness of God (REST)

(5) Forgiveness of sin (RESTORATION)

(2)Sin against God (Rebellion)

(4)Repent and Return

(3)The sternness of God (Discipline/Retribution)

The diagram above shows five things which I want us to consider one after the other;

(1) THE KINDNESS OF GOD (REST)

"Come to me, all who are weary and burdened, and I will give you ***REST****. Take my yoke upon you and learn from me, for I am gentle and humble in heart, and I will give you REST for your soul. For my yoke is easy and my burden is light*". Matt.11:28-30. This is Good News from our Lord Jesus Christ to mankind, and if anyone pays attention to it and accepts Jesus Christ as his Lord and personal savior, the scriptures assure him that ALL PAST SINS COMMITTED WILL BE FORGIVEN AND BE BORN AGAIN.(See Col.2:9-15, 1Cor.6:9-11, 1 Peter 1:23-25)

At this point, God takes all his burdens away and accepts him as a son, son not of natural descent, nor of human decision or a husband's will, but born of God. (John 1:12-13). If this new born child of God obeys and worships Him in truth and in Spirit, he stays in the kindness of God which is having great fellowship with God, and He gives him REST. (Rom.11:22) He talks and prays to God and He answers him. If this believer is able to stay in the kindness of God by keeping His word, he will continue enjoying this great fellowship with God and Satan and his accomplices cannot harm nor touch him. (See Prov.1:33, Luke 6:46-49, 11:28, and 1John 5:18-21)

THE BENEFIT OF ENJOYING THE KINDNESS OF GOD

Christians who are worshipping God in His kindness benefit from these things from Him.

(a) **They enjoy great fellowship with God.**
This great fellowship with God brings believers closer to Him, He listens to their prayers and grants them their requests, because He is pleased with them. **"For the eyes of the Lord are on the RIGHTEOUS and His ears are ATTENTIVE TO THEIR PRAYERS" 1Peter 3:12**. *"And the Lord said to Moses; I WILL DO THE VERY THING YOU HAVE ASKED, BECAUSE I AM PLEASED WITH YOU AND KNOW YOU BY NAME." Exodus 33:17.*

This is one of the benefits of enjoying the kindness of God. God Himself made it clear to Moses, because He was pleased with him, He would do the very thing he had asked. That is GREAT! Certainly, Hannah confirmed this is true and said; "**I prayed for this child, and the Lord has GRANTED me what I asked Him". 1 Sam.1:27**. According to the passage, when Hannah found herself in the kindness of God, she received the very thing she asked for, to confirm what the Lord said in Exodus 33:17 and 1Peter 3:12.

Similarly, believers who are in the kindness of God enjoy great fellowship with Him and their requests are granted no matter what the circumstances. (Phil.4:4-7)

On the other hand, those who are in trials do not receive exactly what they ask from God, but their requests are granted differently. When Jesus was about to face death, He prayed that, that arrangement might be cancelled. Actually, the Father did not grant that request for that plan to be cancelled; instead He strengthened and encouraged Him to face the cross in order for him to save mankind. (See Matthew 26:36-46)

Believers who are in trials for any reason or special assignment in the ministry should advise themselves with this, that no matter how hard they pray, those of their requests which do not match with God's purposes will not be granted in order for God to achieve the reason He sent or allowed that trial came to you. This issue is causing many believers and mighty men of God to see God differently and deny their faith in Him—because they think God has disappointed them. An example of the above scenario occurred in Ghana when a person who felt disappointed by God announced that he was going to place a law suit against God. Watch out! Do not find this amusing. Instead, see what mighty Job said; **"So it profits a man nothing when he tries to please God?" Job 34:9.** What about the great John the Baptist? What did he say? **"Are you the one who was to come, or we should expect someone else?" Luke 7:20.** In fact, John's question suggests he doubted Jesus' reality which himself testified of. (See Matt.3:1-17, John 1:6-8)

Dear reader, in order for you to obtain more knowledge about how God handles such issues; kindly refer to the following texts; Isaiah 46:10-13, 55:6-12, Rev.2:10-11.

(b) **God's gracious hand is on believers who are in His kindness.**
*"Because **the gracious hand of our God was on us**, they brought us Sherebiah, a capable man, from the descendants of Mahli, son of Levi. I was ashamed to ask the king for soldiers and horsemen to protect us from the enemies on the road because we had told the king, **THE GRACIOUS HAND OF GOD IS ON EVERYONE WHO LOOKS TO HIM.**" Ezra 8:18-22.*

According to the passage, all that Ezra was trying to tell us is that, because of the gracious hand of God that was upon him, impossibilities became possibilities in his life. Similarly, if the gracious hand of God is on you, there will be a way for you where there seems to be no way. You will be victorious where people are failing! You will be glorified where people are being disgraced! You will rise where people are falling! You will be successful where people are being defeated! Because the gracious hand of God in believers' life works mysteriously for all who love Him. (See Rom.8:28).

Nehemiah also confirmed this and wrote *"And because of the GRACIOUS HAND OF GOD THAT WAS UPON ME, THE KING GRANT MY REQUEST". Neh.2:8.* Truly, Nehemiah affirmed what Ezra admitted about the gracious hand of God in the life of the believer. He was a slave and so how could such a great king pay attention to him and even grant him his request. It is only the gracious hand of God which does these things. Are you in the kindness of God? Then expect God's gracious hand upon your life to make you a successful believer.

Additionally, Apostle Paul had this to say; **"Consider therefore the KINDNESS AND THE STERNNESS OF GOD; sternness to those who fell, but kindness to you, provided that you continue in His kindness. Otherwise, you will also be cut off". Rom11:22**.

(c) **MERCY:** If any believer is in the kindness of God, it is God's responsibility to show him mercy. As a matter of fact, as long as all believers are flesh and blood, we are bound to commit an offence. However grievous the offenses are, as long as we remain in the kindness of God, He will show us mercy when we are in the wrong unintentionally. (See Zachariah 3:1-10, 1John 5:16-17). Regarding sternness and Kindness refer to Rom.11:22 "*Sternness to those who fell, but KINDNESS to you, provided that you continue in His kindness. Otherwise, you will also be cut off*".

On the other hand, the devil will do everything possible to let you commit an offense, but the mercy of God will keep you and will not allow you to be crushed by the devil. Therefore be on your guard!

(d) **HELP:** If you are in the kindness of God, He will always help you whenever the need arises. He knows you cannot do anything by your might, so He will assist you. (Zach.4:6) If you are weak and cannot pray as you ought to, He will help you. (Rom.8:26). Again, He will not leave you to be over tempted beyond what you can bear. (1Cor.10:13) The devil may obtain permission to torment you with afflictions, but if you are in the kindness of God, He will help you. **"FOR THE EYES OF THE LORD RANGE THROUGHOUT THE EARTH TO STRENGTHEN THOSE WHOSE HEARTS ARE COMMITTED TO HIM". 2Chron.16:9**. "*So we say with confidence;* ***The Lord is my HELPER****; I will not be afraid. What can man (or Satan) do to me?" Heb.13:6.*

Again, if anyone is tired of the struggles in his life and wants to give up on his faith or life, the Lord is always ready to strengthen such a believer. (See Phil.1:27-30) By the following passage, *"HE GIVES STRENGTH TO THE WEARY AND INCREASES THE POWER OF THE WEAK" Isaiah*

40:29. I hope you have realized the reason why we must worship God in His kindness?

(e) **PROTECTION;** God protects His children who are in His kindness from any harm by the devil. Read the following Bible passages to buttress the point raised; **"In the shelter of your PRESENCE you hide them from all human intrigues; you keep them SAFE in your dwelling from accusing tongues" Psalm 31:20**. *"The wicked plot against the righteous and gnash their teeth at them; but the Lord LAUGHS at the wicked, for He knows their day is coming. The wicked draw the sword and bend the bow to bring down the poor and needy, to slay those whose ways are UPRIGHT. BUT THEIR SWORDS WILL PIERCE THEIR OWN HEARTS, AND THEIR BOWS WILL BE BROKEN". Psalm 37:12-15.* **"In God I trust and am not afraid. WHAT CAN MERE HUMAN BEINGS DO TO ME?" Psalm 56:11**. *"We know that anyone born of God does not continue to sin; the one who was born of GOD KEEPS HIM SAFE AND THE EVIL ONE CANNOT HARM HIM". 1John 5:18.* All the passages above show us that the believers who worship God in His kindness enjoy great protection from Him. Whatever the devil plots against them proves futile, because the Almighty God protects them with the shelter of His presence.

Again, the angels of God have been sent out to protect these believers. The following passages confirm it; **"The angels of God ENCAMPED around those who fear Him, and He DELIVERS them". Psalm 34:7**. *"For He will command His angels concerning you to guard you in all your ways, they will lift you up in their hands so that you will not strike your foot against a stone". Psalm 91:11-12.* **"See I am sending an angel ahead of you to guard you along the way and bring you to the place I have prepared". Exod.23:20.** *"ARE NOT ALL ANGELS MINISTERING SPIRIT SENT TO SERVE THOSE WHO WILL INHERIT SALVATION?"* Heb.1:14.

Believers, all these passages tell us that if we are in the kindness of God and about to inherit salvation, then we have a strong protector.

(f) **GUIDE**; *"But when the Spirit of truth comes, He will **GUIDE** you into all truth. He will TELL you what is to come" John 16:13.* Believers who are worshipping God in His kindness are being GUIDED by the Spirit of God into all truth. All truth means anything or any doctrine or teaching which is complicated yet can be revealed by the Holy Spirit to those who are in the kindness of God.

There are many false religions in this world which also claim to have known the truth, but the Lord guides believers in His kindness to the right place. Those who do not fear God and are not worshipping Him in His kindness, have been deceived by these false religions. "**The Spirit clearly says that in later times, some will abandon the faith and follow DECEIVING SPIRIT AND THINGS THOUGHT BY DEMONS. Such TEACHINGS come through hypocritical liars whose consciences have been soared as with hot iron". 1Tim.4:1-2**. *"For such persons are FALSE APOSTLES, DECEITFUL WORKERS, MASQUERADING AS APOSTLES OF CHRIST. AND NO WONDER, FOR SATAN HIMSELF MASQUERADES AS AN ANGEL OF LIGHT. IT IS NOT SURPRISING, THEN, IF HIS SERVANTS ALSO MASQUERADE AS SERVANTS OF RIGHTEOUSNESS. THEIR END WILL BE WHAT THEIR ACTIONS DESERVE." 2Cor.11:13-15.* "**Some have in fact already TURNED AWAY TO FOLLOW SATAN". 1Tim.5:15.**

I hope these powerful passages clearly show us we mingle with people sent by demons to deceive believers with false doctrine, but the believers who are in the kindness of God are lead by the Holy Spirit to the true religion that was established by Himself.

Again, believers who are in the kindness of God are directed by the Spirit of God to know the mind and plans of God for their lives. *"The Lord CONFIDES in those who FEAR Him; He makes His covenant KNOWN TO THEM". Psalm 25:14.* **"However, as it is written; what no eye has seen, what no ear has heard, and what no human mind has conceived—these things God has prepared for those who love Him—for God has REVEALED them to us by His Spirit. The Spirit searches all things, even the DEEP things of God". 1Cor.2:9-10**.

(g) **PROVIDER; God provides for all believers who are worshipping Him in His kindness.** *"And my God will MEET ALL YOUR NEEDS according to His riches in Christ Jesus". Phil.4:19.*

Hannah also realized that it was not by strength that one prevails, but God is the provider. (See 1Sam.2:7-9). Are you in the kindness of God? Be rest assured that God will meet all your needs, no matter what is going on in your life right now. Still believe and relax, because He is faithful and is able to give you anything that can help you to serve Him better. **"The One who calls you is FAITHFUL and He will do it". 1Thess.5:24. (Also see Matt.6:25-34). But check this passage;** *"HIS DIVINE POWER HAS GIVEN US EVERYTHING WE NEED FOR A GODLY LIFE THROUGH OUR KNOWLEDGE OF HIM WHO CALLED US BY HIS OWN GLORY AND GOODNESS". 2Peter 1:3.*

All these good and perfect things are being enjoyed by those believers who are worshipping God in His kindness. Therefore, make it your aim to stay in the kindness of God and you will enjoy all these good and perfect gifts of God. (See James 1:16-17, 2Cor.5:9, Rom.11:22). The only thing you can do to stay in the kindness of God is to OBEY His word all the time. **"But whoever LISTENS TO ME will live in SAFETY, and be at ease without fear of harm". Prov.1:33. (Also see Luke 11:28**)

(2) **REBELLION (SIN)**

The second point in the diagram is rebellion. We have learnt that when a person accepts Jesus Christ and is born again, he directly enjoys the fellowship of God and He gives him rest. Unfortunately, some of these believers ignore this great opportunity of being the sons of the Almighty God. Rather, they rebel against Him after they have received the knowledge of truth. "**Yet they REBELLED AND GRIEVED His Holy Spirit". Isaiah 63:10.**

What we learnt from the book of Numbers showed us that while the Israelites were enjoying the kindness of God, not even the great prophet of God, Balaam and even Satan himself could curse them. Unfortunately, they ignored this great benefit of being in the kindness of God, REBELLED against Him and grieved the Holy Spirit as stated in the book of Isaiah 63:10. Some Christians also behave like the Israelites. When they accept Jesus and are enjoying these benefits, they rebel and do some things which grieve the Holy Spirit. *"And do not GRIEVE the Holy Spirit of God, with whom you were sealed for the day of redemption" Eph.4:30.* (You may read the following texts to see what we do to grieve the Holy Spirit of God; Eph.4:31-32, Gal.5:19-21, 1Cor.6:9-11)

This does not mean that when one accepts Jesus and is born again, he cannot commit an offence. As I told you earlier, as long as we remain human beings, made up of flesh and blood, we are bound to commit offences. The Bible states that; "**Indeed, there is no one on EARTH who does righteous, no one who does what is right and NEVER SINS". Eccl.7:16-20**. *"If we claim to be without sin, we deceive ourselves and the truth is not in us". 1John 1:8.*

The above passages show us that as human beings, we cannot avoid sin completely, but if we commit offense unintentionally, God is faithful and will forgive us and purify us from all unrighteousness. (1John 1:9). On the other hand, this passage does not grant a license to believers to continue sinning after knowing the truth. But what this passage is telling us is that; **"If anyone sees his brother committing a sin that does not lead to death, he should pray and God will give him life. *I refer to those whose sin does not lead to death.* There is a sin that leads to death I am not saying that he should pray about that. ALL WRONG DOING IS SIN, AND THERE IS SIN THAT DOES NOT LEAD TO DEATH". 1 John 5:16-17.**

Again the above passage tells us that believers are bound to commit offenses, but it must be those sins which do not lead to death—condemnation. You may ask, what are sins that lead to death and those that do not lead to death? The simple answer is, any sin committed intentionally and prevalently can lead believers to death—condemnation. *"If we deliberately keep on sinning after we have received the knowledge of truth, NO SACRIFICE (FORGIVENNESS) OF SIN IS LEFT, but only a fearful expectation of JUDGMENT and of raging fire that will consume the enemies of God". Heb.10:16-27.* (Also see James 1:21) "We know also that the son of God has come and has given us UNDERSTANDING, so that we may know him who is true. And we are in him who is true—even in his Son Jesus Christ. He is the true God and eternal life. Therefore, dear children, (CHRISTIANS) KEEP YOURSELVES FROM IDOLS (SINS)". 1John 5:20-21.

(3) THE STERNNESS OF GOD— (RETRIBUTION/DISCIPLINE)

We have just found out from the above lesson that God can be gracious to those believers who commit offences unintentionally, but if any believer rebels against Him and keeps on sinning after this great mercy and grace, that believer will now faces what is called the STERNNESS OF GOD. *"CONSIDER THEREFORE THE KINDNESS AND THE STERNNESS of God; STERNNESS TO THOSE WHO FELL (SINNED), BUT KINDNESS TO YOU PROVIDED THAT YOU CONTINUE IN HIS KINDNESS. OTHERWISE, YOU ALSO WILL BE CUT OFF". Rom. 11:22.*

The sternness of God is when a believer is being disciplined severely by God Himself for sin committed intentionally and has ignored the word of God and keeps on sinning. For example, when God has been gracious to some believers and has blessed them with beautiful and handsome spouses, still, they ignore the word of God and go out to commit serious adultery. This ignites God's wrath and His anger burns against them and He disciplines them severely. *"YET THEY REBELLED AND GRIEVED HIS HOLY SPIRIT. SO HE TURNED AND BECAME THEIR ENEMY, AND HE HIMSELF FOUGHT AGAINST THEM". Isaiah 63:10***.**

According to the passage, when a believer rebels and sins deliberately, God who is supposed to be his redeemer and protector turns against him and becomes his enemy and fights against him. Such a believer, who is facing God's WRATH, may ignorantly set his focus on Satan and start throwing bomb and fire at him in prayers!

The Israelites faced this when they rebelled against God after He had protected them from curses and denounces. On that day, twenty-four thousand (24,000) people died by God's wrath. This is the STERNNESS OF GOD—the harsh discipline of God to His ungrateful children, who willfully refuse to stay in His kindness. *"IN YOUR STRUGGLE AGAINST SIN, YOU HAVE NOT YET RESISTED TO THE POINT OF SHEDDING YOUR BLOOD. AND HAVE YOU COMPLETELY FORGOTTEN THIS WORD OF ENCOURAGEMENT THAT ADDRESSES YOU AS CHILDREN? IT SAYS, MY SON, DO NOT MAKE LIGHT OF THE*

LORD'S DISCIPLINE, AND DO NOT LOSE HEART WHEN HE REBUKES YOU, *BECAUSE THE LORD DISCIPLINES THOSE HE LOVES, AND HE CHASTENS EVERYONE HE ACCEPTS AS HIS CHILD" Heb.12:4-6.* (Heb.12:4-11)

Let's find out what happens to believers in the STERNNESS of God.

(a) **THEIR PRAYERS AND REQUEST ARE NOT GRANTED BY GOD**; *"SINCE YOU IGNORED ALL MY ADVICE AND WOULD NOT ACCEPT MY REBUKE,* ***I IN TURN WILL LAUGH AT YOUR DISASTER,*** *I WILL MOCK WHEN CALAMITY OVERTAKES YOU, AND THEY WILL CALL ON ME AND* ***I WILL NOT ANSWER;*** *THEY WILL LOOK FOR ME AND* ***WILL NOT FIND ME,*** *SINCE THEY HATED KNOWLEDGE AND DID NOT CHOOSE TO FEAR THE LORD". Prov.1:25-29*

This passage illustrates that believers in the STERNNESS of God are being punished for their deliberate disobedience to God. When you accept Jesus Christ, the bible teaches you that God hates divorce; nevertheless some believers go ahead and divorce their spouses. (See Mal.2:14-16). Again the bible instructs us that our bodies are the temples of God which is the dwelling place of the Holy Spirit so we should keep it holy; but, others go ahead and degrade their bodies with adultery and fornication. (See 1Cor.6:18-20) *"YOU WERE BOUGHT AT A PRICE. THEREFORE, HONOR GOD WITH YOUR BODIES". 1Cor.6:20.* God wants love and unity to exist within the body of believers, but the disobedient believers are envying each other and causing divisions among themselves even in the church. (See John 17:20-26, Gal.5:26, Titus 3:9-10).

Again, there are other things our loving God wants us to avoid and separate ourselves from but some of us still ignore these directives and keep on doing those contraindicated things to provoke God. (See 1Cor.6:9-11, Rom.1:21-32, Gal.5:19-21). This behavior plunges the believer into the STERNNESS of God, which is not an easy nor pleasant experience for the believer in that situation—God in turn as a result of your disobedience, refuses to answer your prayer in times of great trouble. The worst of it all is He laughs at you in the time of distress. (See Prov.1:25-29).

The sternness of God is nothing any believer would elect to experience simply because it is not easy to bear the wrath of God. God told Moses that; *"I will do the VERY THING YOU HAVE ASKED, because I am pleased with you and I know you by name".* Exod.33:17. This happened when Moses was in the kindness of God, but when he disobeyed Him and found himself in the sternness of God, everything changed. "**But because of you, the Lord is angry with me and will NOT LISTEN to me. This is enough, the Lord said, DO NOT SPEAK TO ME ABOUT THIS MATTER ANY MORE". Deut.3:26 (Deut.3:23-29**).

We can infer from the above scenario that it is dangerous to serve the Lord in His sternness. Whereas the prayers of the believers in His kindness are accepted and granted quickly, that of the believers in the sternness of God become useless. *"FOR THE EYES OF THE LORD ARE ON THE RIGHTEOUS AND HIS EARS ARE* ***ATTENTIVE TO THEIR PRAYERS****, BUT THE FACE OF THE LORD* ***IS AGAINST THOSE WHO DO EVIL****". 1Peter 3:12.*

As a matter of fact, ministers of God who have been trained in Bible schools are not encouraged to preach about this topic—THE STERNNESS OF GOD. The reason being that, it puts fear in some believers especially the new converts and confuses them of their position in the Lord. This is the time I have been commanded to let you know the truth in order that you will not continue hailing stones and bombs at Satan for all your predicaments.

(b) **GOD HIMSELF FIGHTS AGAINST THEM;** *"Yet they rebelled and grieved His Holy Spirit, so He turned and became their enemy and* ***He (God) Himself FOUGHT against them****". Isaiah 63:10.*

God does not let any of His disobedient children go entirely unpunished. His disciplinary action seem to be too harsh for us, that is why the Apostle Paul themed it; **'THE STERNNESS OF GOD'**. Generally, the sternness of God is not easy to bear, because our God who is expected to protect us from the threats of the devil has now TURNED and has become an enemy to those erring believers. *"I WILL NOT COMPLETELY DESTROY YOU. I WILL DISCIPLINE YOU BUT ONLY WITH JUSTICE, I WILL NOT LET YOU GO ENTIRELY UNPUNISHED. THIS IS WHAT THE LORD SAYS, YOUR WOUND IS INCURABLE, YOUR INJURY*

BEYOND HEALING. THERE IS NO-ONE TO PLEAD YOUR CAUSE, NO REMEDY FOR YOUR SORE, NO HEALING FOR YOU. I HAVE STRUCK YOU AS AN ENEMY WOULD AND PUNISHED YOU AS WOULD THE CRUEL, BECAUSE YOUR GUILT IS SO GREAT AND SINS SO MANY. WHY DO YOU CRY OUT OVER YOUR WOUND, AND PAIN THAT HAS NO CURE? BECAUSE OF YOUR GREAT GUILT AND MANY SINS, I HAVE DONE THESE THINGS TO YOU". Jer.30:11-16.

I need to emphasize that worshipping God in His sternness (wrath) is not an easy task to bear as you can see from this passage. **"I will not let you go entirely UNPUNISHED, this is what the Lord says". Jer.30:11**. Therefore, all attempts must be made by the believer to avoid falling into the sternness of God because *"IT IS A DREADFUL THING TO FALL INTO THE HANDS OF THE LIVING GOD". Heb.10:31.*

(c) **BELIEVERS IN THE STERNNESS OF GOD LOSE THEIR FELLOSHIP WITH GOD**;

"Why should any living man complain when punished for his sins? WE HAVE SINNED AND REBELLED AND YOU HAVE NOT FORGIVEN. You have covered yourself with anger and pursued us; You have slain WITHOUT PITY. You have covered yourself with cloud so that no PRAYER can get through". Lam.3:39-44.

The above passage confirms the point that erring believers sin and keep on rebelling, consequently God also does not forgive them without first disciplining them. Therefore God covers Himself with a cloud and anger so that He may not see how the destroying angels are tormenting them. *"AND DO NOT GRUMBLE, AS SOME OF THEM DID—AND WERE KILLED BY THE DESTROYING ANGELS". 1Cor.10:10.* **"Why should God be ANGRY at what you say and DESTROY the work of your hand?" Eccl.5:6**. (Also see 2 Sam.24:15-17, 1 Sam.18:10-12)

I know that these passages are not good news to believers, and they are not happy to be exposed to such teachings but they are real and it is happening to erring believers everyday. Their fellowship with God has been broken and God has turned against them and has become their enemy and has sent the destroying angels out to wage war in their life. Since these believers do not know what exactly is happening to them, they rather turn to attack the devil for their predicaments.

Let's consider the story of Ahab, the Israelite king in the Bible. He rebelled against God and He got angry with him and wanted to punish him with death. According to the scriptures, God sat down on His Throne to discuss this issue with His heavenly hosts. You can read the full story from the scriptures; 2 Chron.18:1-34. I want to give you this small portion of the story to support this point; "**And the Lord said who will ENTICE Ahab, king of Israel into attacking Ramoth Gilead and going to have his DEATH there? One suggested this and another suggested that. Finally, a SPIRIT came forward, stood before the Lord and said, 'I will ENTICE him', by what means? The Lord asked. (Please pay attention to what is happening to erring believers and what tactic that spirit deployed to succeed in this assignment) I WILL GO AND BE A LYING SPIRIT IN THE MOUTH OF ALL HIS PROPHETS. GOD SAID, YOU WILL SUCCEED IN ENTICE HIM. GO AND DO IT". 2Chron.18:19-21.**

This spirit of God was mandated to go and do anything within his capability to make sure Ahab would go to that war to encounter his demise. Surely that spirit was able to ENTICE Ahab to ignore the advice and true prophesy of God's anointed prophet and attacked Ramoth Gilead, which resulted in his death there at the design of his supposed redeemer and protector (GOD). 1Chron.18:28-34.

I am sure believers will advise themselves with this lesson, because it is easy to conclude that it was the devil who deceived Ahab and hardened his heart to ignore the man of God's prophesy and hence his death. Again, this should also be a lesson for those who still do not believe that there are false prophets among us sent to deceive believers who are perishing. (See 2Thess.2:9-12)

Another example is about Saul who pleased God and was chosen by Him to be the first king of Israel. He also disobeyed God and fell into the hands of the living God. (Heb.10:31) The scriptures say; "The next day AN EVIL SPIRIT FROM GOD (NOT SATAN) CAME FORCEFULLY UPON SAUL". 1Sam.18:10. Believers should know that our merciful God has His own DESTROYING ANGELS who He always sends out to discipline His erring believers. (Note; the erring believers are believers who intentionally disobey the word of God and keep on sinning—it is called REBELLION.)

Again, God found David and was pleased with him and sent Samuel to anoint him to succeed Saul's throne as the second king of Isreal. Unfortunately, this man who was loved and chosen by God committed different kinds of offences, and God also punished him in different ways. On one occasion, He sent one of the DESTROYING ANGELS to kill his people. You can read this story from 1 Chron. 21:1-30. But let me share this portion with you; "*So the Lord sent a plague on Israel from that time designated and seventy thousand of the people from Dan to Beersheba died. WHEN THE ANGEL STRETCHED OUT HIS HAND TO DESTROY JERUSALEM, THE LORD WAS GRIEVED BECAUSE OF THE CALAMITY AND SAID TO THE ANGEL WHO WAS AFFLICTING THE PEOPLE. ENOUGH! WITHDRAW YOUR HAND. THE ANGEL OF THE LORD (not the angel of Satan) WAS THEN AT THE THRESHING-FLOOR OF ARAUNAH THE JEBUSITE. WHEN DAVID SAW THE ANGEL WHO WAS STRIKING DOWN THE PEOPLE, HE SAID TO THE LORD, 'I AM THE ONE WHO HAS SINNED AND WRONGED. THESE ARE BUT SHEEP. WHAT HAVE THEY DONE? LET YOUR HAND FALL UPON ME AND MY FAMILY, but do not let this plague remain on your people". 1 Chron. 21:15-17.*

If believers do not know that God has His own DESTROYING ANGELS which are sent to discipline erring believers, I hope this lesson has revealed it to you. According to the passage, King David saw one of them who was STRIKING HIS PEOPLE TO DEATH. We can see from the passage that, although David saw the angel who was afflicting his people, he did not confront him or Satan, but he dealt with God—knowing very well that if he had not been sent by God, he could not have had the opportunity to torment them. When God accepted David's plea, He then COMMANDED the destroying angel to cease his operation.

I hope this lesson has shown you that believers are dealing with God but not with Satan in their predicaments. So we should carefully investigate why we find ourselves in our peculiar situations. When you find out that you have done wrong, accept your fault and repent—this leads us to the next point in the diagram.

(4) REPENT AND RETURN

The fourth point shown in the diagram is **REPENT AND RETURN**. We have learnt that when a believer disobeys the word of God and continues to sin, he falls into the hands of the living God which is termed as 'THE STERNNESS OF GOD'. (Rom.11:22, Heb.10:31) In this state, we found out that God becomes an enemy to His erring children and fights against them with problems to teach them a good lesson. *"SO THEN, THOSE WHO SUFFER ACCORDING TO GOD'S WILL SHOULD COMMIT THEMSELVES TO THEIR FAITHFUL CREATOR AND CONTINUE TO DO GOOD". 1Peter4:19.*

When a believer finds himself in this state in Christianity, what he must do is to REPENT from his sin and RETURN to God, because he is still a child of God.

The story of the Prodigal son is not a real incident, but it is an example of a repentant condition of the believer. (See Luke 15:11-32). In fact, that son behaved extremely bad, but no matter how great he offended his father, the father did not forsake him, rather, he was waiting to see his son again which did happened. I know most of my readers know everything about this story, the Father represents our heavenly Father—God, and the prodigal son also represents an erring believer who has gone astray. This same scenario applies to any believer who is in the STERNNESS OF GOD. The believer who has sinned and is under God's discipline needs to REPENT AND RETURN TO GOD. (See Heb.12:4-11)

The Bible says; **"My people are destroyed from the lack of knowledge".** Hosea 4:6. When these erring believers find themselves in the sternness of God, instead of repenting from their sins and returning to their loving Father, they rather seek deliverance from other sources which help Satan and his accomplices to steal their minds from God and it ends them into death. *"GODLY SORROW BRINGS REPENTANCE THAT LEADS TO SALVATION AND LEAVES NO REGRET, BUT WORLDLY SORROW BRINGS D E A T H". 2 Cor.7:10.*

When a believer deliberately sins, there is a break up of his fellowship with God as we have discussed earlier, but the relationship between Father and son still remains unless he chooses to give up and backslides to the world.

Instead of the believer reverting to the world, he must rather repent and return to the Father, who does not give up on mankind no matter the magnitude of the crimes they have committed. The scripture below shows us what we must do as believers whenever we are caught deep in wrong doings or sin. **"Let the wicked forsakes his ways and the evil man his thought. Let him TURN TO THE LORD AND HE WILL HAVE MERCY ON HIM, AND TO OUR GOD, FOR HE WILL FREELY PARDON". Isaiah 55:7.** *"Why should any living man complain when he is PUNISHED FOR HIS SINS? Let us examine our ways and test them,* ***and let us RETURN TO THE LORD****. Let us lift our hearts and hands to God in heaven and say,* ***WE HAVE SINNED AND REBELLED*** *AND YOU HAVE NOT FORGIVEN. You have covered yourself with ANGER and pursued us; you have SLAIN WITHOUT PITY. You have covered yourself with a cloud so that no prayer can get through". Lam.3:39-44.*

We have now learnt that our loving Father in heaven can be revengeful of our sins, but when we accept our faults and return to Him, He will forgive us and accept us as His sons again. Are you in the sternness of God? You need **REPENTANCE AND NOT DELIVERANCE!** The Holy Spirit gives us power to deliver people who are under the bondage of the devil, but Christians can never be found under the devil's bondage. Thus, if you are a Christian and you are experiencing some difficulties in life, do not set your eyes on the devil and expect to be delivered from his hand. As a matter of fact, you received your deliverance the very day you accepted Jesus Christ as your Lord and personal savior—the scriptures describes that experience as being "CROSSED OVER FROM DEATH TO LIFE"! It also means you have crossed over from the bondage of the devil to the Great Kingdom of God. In fact, according to the scriptures, you were added to the body of Christ the very day you were baptized.

Certainly, I am writing all these to help believers to carefully examine themselves properly and see if they are truly Christians who have crossed over from death to eternal life and have been delivered from the hands of Satan, so as to not deceive themselves with the name of Jesus Christ. Because anyone who has been born again has already been delivered once and for all!

Hopefully the readers of this book have realized that believers need to **REPENT AND NOT TO BE DELIVERED**! We must distinguish these two words very well—**DELIVERANCE AND REPENTANCE.** Deliverance is for people who are possessed with demons and people who are under their control. If I may ask, are Christians under the devil's bondage? Definitely NOT! What does the scripture say? "**There is now no condemnation for those who are in CHRIST JESUS—HALELUJAH!**" **Rom.8:1(Rom.8:1-4.)**

Therefore, if you are a Christian and things are not going on in your life as expected, just examine your ways to know if you have done any wrong against God as stated in Lamentations 3:39-44, because whether you are ignorant or not, He has said, no-one can go ENTIRELY UNPUNISHED for any sin committed. (See Jeremiah 30:11).

On the contrary, REPENTANCE is for believers who have sinned and are in the sternness of God. Believers who are in the sternness of God should come to their senses just like the prodigal son did. (Luke 15:11-32). Therefore, believers should not confuse these two experiences—Deliverance and Repentance. Again, ministers and church leaders are not to deliver believers who are in the hands of the living God for discipline—it is impossible, because; **"IT IS A DREADFUL THING TO FALL INTO THE HANDS OF THE LIVING GOD". Heb.10:31.** *"And you have forgotten that word of encouragement that addresses you as sons, my son, do not make light of the Lord's DISCIPLINE, and do not lose heart when He REBUKES you, because the Lord disciplines those He loves and PUNISHED EVERYONE HE ACCEPTS AS A SON. Endure hardship as discipline, for God is treating you as sons. For what son is not disciplined (and everyone undergoes discipline) then you are ILLEGITIMATE CHILDREN AND NOT TRUE SONS. Moreover we have all had human fathers who discipline us and we respected them for that. How much more should we submit to the Father of our spirit and LIVE! Our fathers discipline us for a little while as they thought best; Bur God disciplines us for our good that we may share in His holiness. No discipline seems pleasant at the time, but PAINFUL. Later on, however, it produces a harvest of righteousness and peace for those who have been trained by it". Heb.12:5-11.*

God does not let us go entirely unpunished, but He makes sure everyone receives the requisite discipline for our actions so that we can also share in His Holiness. **"BUT GOD DISCIPLINES US FOR OUR GOOD THAT WE MAY SHARE IN HIS HOLINESS. LATER ON IT**

PRODUCES A HARVEST OF RIGHTEOUSNESS AND PEACE FOR THOSE WHO HAVE BEEN TRAINED BY IT". Heb.12:10-11. *"SO THEN, THOSE WHO SUFFER ACCORDING TO GOD'S WILL SHOULD COMMIT THEMSELVES TO THEIR FAITHFUL CREATOR AND CONTINUE TO DO GOOD". 1Peter 4:19.*

My dear reader, I hope after you have read this topic, you will no longer seek to be delivered while you must repent and return to God. He is ever ready to receive and freely pardon His erring children who have submissively been trained through discipline. (See Lam.3:39-44, Isaiah 55:6-12, 63:10, Jer.30:11).

(5) RESTORATION (FORGIVENNESS OF SIN)

The fifth point shown in the diagram is RESTORATION—FORGIVENNESS OF SIN. We previously learnt that if we recognize our offences, repent and return to God, He freely forgives us and happily accepts us as sons again. (See Luke 15:11-32). This state in Christianity is called—RESTORATION. A state where your sins have been forgiven and you are waiting to enter into the KINDNESS OF GOD—the first point in the diagram, which looks like a circle. The life of believers is rotating before God, it starts with an unbeliever being saved by God's grace and mercy, then he falls into sin and rebels against Him, then God disciplines him, then he recognizes his sins, repents and returns to Him, who accepts his plea and forgives him. When a believer is being forgiven of his sin, he then gets another chance to be in the kindness of God. Here he enjoys great fellowship with God so when he prays, God listens to him and grants him his requests. This is the point every believer wishes to be at in their relationship with God.

Sadly, it is at this moment that most of the erring believers backslide and turn away from God. Because they have been taught that when they confess their sins and sin no more, God will forgive them and cleanse them from all unrighteousness. (Isaiah 55:7, 1John 1:9) Therefore, when they repent and receive the forgiveness of their sins, they want to enter into the kindness of God and have great fellowship with Him straight away. (See 1Peter 3:12, 2Chron.16:9, Exod.33:17, Ezra 8:18, 22, Neh.2:8, 1Sam.1:27) But before one can move from restoration to REST (The Kindness of

God), he needs to exhibit perseverance and wait a little while in that state of restoration, so that he can be properly trained in order not to commit those offences again. (See Heb.12:10-11, 1Peter 4:1-6, 19)

It is at this state that prophet Micah prophesied and said; **"But as for me, I watch in hope for the Lord, I WAIT for God my Savior, my God will hear me. Do not gloat over me, my enemy! Though I have FALLEN, I will rise. Though I sit in darkness, the Lord will be my light. Because I have SINNED against Him, I will bear the Lord's WRATH, (THE STERNNESS OF GOD) until He pleads my case and establishes my right. HE WILL BRING ME OUT INTO THE LIGHT; (REST-KINDNESS OF GOD) I will see his righteousness. Then my enemy will see it and will be covered with SHAME, she who said where the Lord is your God". Micah 7:7-10.**

Prophet Micah realized that he deserved to be punished and thus accepted the blame for his condition. This is what is called RESTORATION! A state where the believer accepts God's discipline in good faith and perseveres until God Himself restores him into His kindness (REST). *"So do not throw away your confidence; it will be richly rewarded. YOU NEED TO PERSEVERE so that when you have done the will of God, you will receive what he has promised. For in just a very little while, He who is coming will come and will not DELAY. BUT MY RIGHTEOUS WILL LIVE BY FAITH. AND IF HE SHRINKS BACK, I WILL NOT BE PLEASED WITH HIM. BUT WE ARE NOT OF THOSE WHO SHRINK BACK AND ARE DESTROYED, BUT OF THOSE WHO BELIEVE AND ARE SAVED". Heb.10:35-39.*

This passage tells us what we must do if anyone finds himself in the restoration. A state where your sins have been forgiven and covered, (Psalm 32:1-3), what you need is PERSEVERANCE that can help you to wait patiently for God Himself to restore you back to His kindness, where every believer delights to reside.

Some believers cannot wait for God to restore them into His kindness, and for this reason they seek help from self professed "Men of God", 'Prophet of God', but they are not! (Read the following passages; 2Cor.11:13-15, Rev.2:9, 3:9, 2Thess.2:9-12.) I therefore urge those believers who seek quick restoration from other sources to wait patiently for God Himself to restore them for the sake of their salvation. For this reason the Prophet Isaiah wrote; *"YET THE LORD LONGS TO BE GRACIOUS TO YOU; HE RISES TO SHOW YOU COMPASSION. FOR THE LORD IS A GOD OF JUSTICE. BLESSED ARE ALL WHO WAIT FOR HIM". Isaiah30:18.*

Another point is that if you find yourself in this state, try to pray earnestly and effectively to remind God to save you from that unwanted situation. Isaiah again wrote that; "**REVIEW THE PAST FOR ME, LET US ARGUE THE MATTER TOGETHER; STATE THE CASE FOR YOUR INNOCENCE". Isaiah 43:26**. *"O PEOPLE OF ZION WHO LIVE IN JERUSALEM, YOU WILL WEEP NO MORE. HOW GRACIOUS HE WILL BE WHEN YOU CRY FOR HELP! AS SOON AS HE HEARS, HE WILL ANSWER YOU". Isaiah 30:19.*

When the Apostle Paul added his voice to this he said; *"Do not be anxious about anything but in everything by PRAYER AND PETITION, with thanksgiving, present your request to God and the peace of God which transcends all understanding, will guard your hearts and your mind in Christ Jesus"*. Phil.4:4-7. If believers in this state fail to pray effectively, Satan can utilize that opportunity to steal their minds from God and deceive them to seek solutions for their problems from other sources. We must rely on God alone to save us from the problems we may encounter. "**You will keep in perfect peace him whose mind is STEADFAST, because he trusts in you. Trust in the Lord for ever (until He saves you) for the Lord is the Rock Eternally". Isaiah 26:3-5.**

Dear reader if God Himself saves you, it is eternal, but if those agents of the devil who masquerade as apostles and ministers of God save you, they exchange your problem for your salvation. (See 2Thess. 2:9-12, 2Cor.11:13-15) Believers need to be mindful of the fact that Satan does not control their lives although he may be controlling the world. If you keep yourself from; the cravings of the sinful nature, the lust of the eyes and boasting about your gains and what you do, you will be able to overcome him. Remember that such a behavior does not come from the Father, but from him who is controlling the world, and he uses these as traps to lure us to rebel against our heavenly Father. (John 14:30, 1John 2:15-17, 5:18-21). The devil therefore gains grounds to accuse the believers before the Father because of the sins they have committed, (Zach.3:1-10), and if we are disciplined by God, he uses that opportunity to deceive and put those vulnerable believers into his grasp and in bondage causing them all kinds of problems. This explains why although some people in the church may profess to be Christians yet may either be possessed or under the control of demons.

Apostle Paul and John wanted believers to understand this principle that Jesus Christ did not take away the controlling of the world from Satan, but He SAVED us from his bondage and seated us with Him in heavenly realms in order that in the coming ages, He might show the incomparable riches of His grace expressed in HIS KINDNESS TO US IN CHRIST JESUS. (See Eph.2:1-10, John 14:30, 1John 5:18-21). This is what Christ Jesus had done for us, therefore anyone who claims to be a child of God should try to keep himself from idols (sins-1John5:21).

My dear reader, all these references clearly show that as a child of the Almighty God, Satan or any of his accomplices cannot harm you, unless you get out from God's protection. Once you are in Christ Jesus who is able to protect you from the devil's treat, bear in mind that whatever happens in your life must have originated from your heavenly Father, because He is in-charge of your life, but not the devil. Do not let Satan feel proud that he is able to torment you. For if it is possible for the devil to cause havoc to us, then we might be in great trouble if we have to constantly deal with such a wicked creature. He has no mercy for mankind. Look at what he is doing to unbelievers, the problems he is using them to cause to each other and the world in general. If he is the one controlling our lives, he would not even give us food to eat, because we have persistently refused to serve him. But thanks be to God Almighty, who has been our provider. (See Ezekiel 36:29-32, Phil.4:19, 2 Peter 1:3-4).

When you read the Bible texts I have provided above especially Ezekiel, it tells us about how God was able to save His people, and would not allow them to suffer a famine. In this case, should these people who would only endure famine as a result of their disobedience to God blame the devil for bringing famine on them? Definitely not! Because it is not the devil who feeds them hence he cannot bring any famine on them. It is only the Lord who feeds them who can bring a famine on them.

Dear reader, it is worth noting that our God has enough strength and power to protect you from the hands of the devil. (Heb.12:28-29)

Therefore, we should not give credit to Satan and his accomplices in any of our problems, trials and tribulations. Accept that anything you are experiencing has been allowed by your heavenly Father who does not change like shifting shadows. He may permit them to come to you either to discipline you for the offences committed for which you must not go entirely UNPUNISHED, or to train you to be strong in your faith. (You may confirm this from the following texts; Isaiah 63:10, Jer.30:11-15, Lam.3:37-44, Rom.8:17-18, Phil.1:27-30, 1Peter 1:6-7, 4:12-16, Rev.2:10). *"AND THE GOD OF ALL GRACE, WHO CALLED YOU TO HIS ETERNAL GLORY IN CHRIST, AFTER YOU HAVE SUFFERED A LITTLE WHILE WITH HIMSELF RESTORE YOU AND MAKE YOU STRONG, FIRM AND STEADFAST". 1Peter 5:10.*

We as believers are dealing with God but not Satan, so we must desist from blaming Satan and his accomplices for all our problems. Instead we should repent and pray to God who is in control of our lives for the forgiveness of our sins rather than attending prayer camps and turning to other sources for deliverance.

Dear reader I want to caution you not to hastily presume that any believer who is facing some difficulties in life has sinned and is probably facing the wrath of God. Bear in mind that not all of them are facing God's discipline, because Job faced all kinds of trials but was not in any way being disciplined by God for any wrong doing. (See Job 1:1-6, 2:1-10.) Joseph was also put into prison when he tried to avoid adultery and run away from sin. (See Gen.39:1-23). Again, the scriptures did not state that Hannah had committed an abortion that is why God CLOSED HER WOMB. (See 1Sam.1:1-8). But let's consider this passage; *"BUT TO HANNAH HE GAVE A DOUBLE PORTION BECAUSE HE LOVED HER, AND THE LORD HAD CLOSED HER WOMB. BECAUSE THE LORD HAD CLOSED HANNAH'S WOMB, HER RIVAL KEPT PROVOKING HER IN ORDER TO IRRITATE HER". 1Sam.1:4-5.*

Undoubtedly, what happened to Hannah is still happening to some believers these days. I can recount the testimonies of some believing couples who seemingly were barren several years after their marriage and the kind of ordeal they encountered at the hands of their fellow believers. According to some of the people in these situations it is such pressures that push them especially, the women among them to look for solution from other sources beside our Only Sovereign God. There is a good lesson we can consider from Hannah's action. When the devil hired her rival to increase her woes, she did not attempt to seek deliverance from any human being, but she took the problem straight to the Almighty God. She might have known that once she was a child of God, it is His responsibility to ensure that she was not to be put to shame. **"AS THE SCRIPTURES SAY; ANYONE WHO BELIEVES IN HIM WILL NEVER BE PUT TO SHAME". Rom.10:11**.

Similarly, there are some people who have mingled with us and professed to be Christians, but rather have been sent by the devil to take advantage of our unique circumstances, and lure us to ignore the word of God which guides us and look for solutions at questionable places. *"FOR CERTAIN INDIVIDUALS WHOSE CONDEMNATION WAS WRITTEN ABOUT LONG AGO HAVE SECRETLY SLIPPED IN AMONG YOU. THEY ARE UNGODLY PEOPLE, WHO PERVERT THE GRACE OF OUR GOD INTO A LICENSE FOR IMMORALITY AND DENY JESUS CHRIST OUR ONLY SOVEREIGN AND LORD". Jude 4.*

I hope this lesson is going to help some believers to be stable in their faith in God, and will not allow these agents of the devil to confound and outwit them due to their inability to bear children yet. **"I AM CONFIDENT IN THE LORD THAT YOU WILL TAKE NO OTHER VIEW. THE ONE WHO IS THROWING YOU INTO CONFUSION WILL HAVE TO PAY THE PENALTY, WHOEVER HE MAY BE". Gal.5:10**. These believers should remind and encourage themselves with the word of God that Sarah, Rebecca, Rachel, Elizabeth and other mighty women of God in the scriptures did not commit any crime such as an abortion, etc. but the scriptures confirm that the Lord CLOSED their wombs for the very reason best know to Him alone. Therefore, be on your guard about such people among us!

Dear reader, I am on this note about to outline for some of the deeds which the devil lures believers to commit against God that brings His wrath against them; **"IN ORDER THAT SATAN MIGHT NOT OUTWIT US, FOR WE ARE NOT UNAWARE OF HIS SCHEMES". 2 Cor.2:11**.

The remaining chapters treat those subjects.

CHAPTER 4

THE LAW AND THE COMMANDMENT

Jesus Christ came to this earth to save mankind from the bondage and dominion of the devil and to show us the way to the Father. *"Jesus answered; I am the WAY, THE TRUTH AND THE LIFE. No-one comes to the Father except THROUGH ME". John 14:6.* Truly, He is the only one appointed by the Father to lead mankind into His kingdom, but He faced antagonism from the Pharisees and Sadducees. This is because they thought He was trying to destroy the law and change the way they had been taught to worship God by Moses. He then replied them and said; **"Do not think that I have come to abolish the law and the prophets: I have not come to abolish but to fulfill them". Matt.5:17.** He even continued that if anyone breaks the least of the COMMANDMENT, that person will be condemned; instead, everyone must obey, practice and teach others to practice what the law says. (See Matt.5:19)

Somehow, the law was very complicated and the people could not obey them accordingly, so He gathered all of them together and divided them into two parts. The first part was named; 'THE FIRST AND THE GREATEST COMMANDMENT', and the other part was also known as; 'THE SECOND COMMANDMENT'. At some points the Pharisees themselves enquired about the law from Him. They brought a woman to be judged by Jesus Himself when they caught her with their 'naked eyes' committing an act of adultery. After Jesus' judgment, though the woman had truly committed adultery, yet He set her free. Because they were baffled by the law they gathered courage and came to ask Jesus a very important question; *"TEACHER, WHICH IS THE GREATEST COMMANDMENT IN THE LAW? Jesus replied; LOVE the Lord your God with all your HEART and with all your SOUL and with all your MIND and with all your STRENGTH. This is the first and the greatest commandment. The second is like it; LOVE your neighbor as yourself. ALL THE LAW AND THE PROPHETS HANG ON THESE TWO COMMANDMENTS. There is no commandment greater than these".* Matt.22:34-40. (Mark 12:28-31)

The passage shows that our Lord Jesus Christ did not ABOLISH the law, but He made them a commandment and said, all the law and the prophets hang on these two commandments. Thus, if anyone thinks there is no more law so he can worship God anyhow, that believer will be judged. (Matt.5:19). He continued that those who are establishing their churches and teaching their congregation different doctrines will be judged. The fact that Jesus had made the law as a commandment does not give us a chance to throw them away and worship God anyhow. This is the work of the devil to steal our hearts and minds from worshipping God properly and be saved.

Jesus Christ redeemed us from under the law and we become heirs of the Father. *"But when the time had fully come, God sent His Son born of a woman under the LAW TO REDEEM THOSE UNDER THE LAW THAT WE MIGHT RECEIVE THE FULL RIGHT OF SONS. Because you are sons, God sent the Spirit of His Son into your heart, the Spirit who calls out, Abba Father. SO YOU ARE NO LONGER A SLAVE, BUT A SON; AND SINCE YOU ARE A SON, GOD HAS MADE YOU ALSO AN HEIR'.* Gal.4:4-7. (Also see Gal.3:1-29, 4:1-30, 5:1-25.)

Some churches and Christians think that a group of believers from other denominations are breaking the law, because they do not worship God on a particular day like Saturday, or because they eat some foods or animals which are forbidden by the law. In response to this, the Apostle Paul was very angry with those who still wanted to continually worship God under the law, despite His numerous attempts to teach them we are no longer worshipping God under the Law. Let's consider this passage; *"FORMERLY, WHEN YOU DID NOT KNOW GOD, YOU WERE SLAVE TO THOSE WHO BY NATURE ARE NOT GODS. BUT NOW THAT YOU KNOW GOD—OR RATHER ARE KNOWN BY GOD—HOW IS IT THAT*

YOU ARE TURNING BACK TO THOSE WEAK AND MISERABLE PRINCIPLES? DO YOU WISH TO BE ENSLAVED BY THEM ALL OVER AGAIN? YOU ARE OBSERVING SPECIAL DAYS AND MONTHS AND SEASONS AND YEARS! I FEAR FOR YOU, THAT SOMEHOW I HAVE WASTED MY EFFORT. TELL ME, YOU WHO WANT TO BE UNDER THE LAW, ARE YOU NOT AWARE OF WHAT THE LAW SAYS?" Gal.4:8-11, 21.

We can see from the passage that Paul was annoyed with those believers who did not understand this simple fact in Christianity and still wanted to worship God under the law. He had already explained to them that they were no more under the law, because Jesus Christ had taken them from under the law. He therefore rebuked those disciples who wanted to force the Gentiles to worship God under the law. *"WHEN I SAW THAT THEY WERE NOT ACTING IN LINE WITH THE TRUTH IN THE GOSPEL, I SAID TO PETER INFRONT OF THEM ALL. HOW IS IT THEN, THAT YOU FORCE GENTILE TO FOLLOW THE JEWISH CUSTOM? WE WHO ARE JEWISH BY BIRTH AND NOT GENTILE SINNERS KNOW THAT A MAN IS NOT JUSTIFIED BY OBSERVING THE LAW, BUT BY FAITH IN JESUS CHRIST, SO WE TOO HAVE PUT OUR FAITH IN CHRIST AND NOT BY OBSERVING THE LAW.* ***BECAUSE BY OBSERVING THE LAW, NO-ONE WILL BE JUSTIFIED".*** *Gal.2:14-16.*

After the death of Christ Jesus, people who believe in Jesus Christ are redeemed from under the law, because according to the last sentence of the passage we just read, it says; '**BY OBSERVING THE LAW, OR WORSHIPPING GOD UNDER THE LAW, NO-ONE WILL BE JUSTIFIED (AND FOR THAT MATTER, NO-ONE CAN BE SAVED).**' Gal.2:16. When Jesus made the law a commandment, it became easy to worship God because the fears of being stoned or punished for committing a particular sin were eliminated from Christianity. As a matter of fact, if the law is still active in Christianity, then what are the benefits of the death of Christ Jesus?

However some Christians are still confused about how Jesus' commandment works; as a result believers have divergent views and interpretations to them. For instance, a while back, there was a great argument among some believers about the Sabbath day, the law and some animals which the law forbids believers to eat. In fact, I do not understand why some believers allow themselves to be carried away by any teaching at all. (Eph.4:14) Because Jesus Christ who is our Lord—means Master—Teacher, made it clear that all the law hang on these two commandments. This also surprised the apostle and he asked; **'HOW IS IT THAT YOU ARE TURNING BACK TO THOSE WEAK AND MISERABLE PRINCIPLES? DO YOU WISH TO BE ENSLAVED BY THEM ALL OVER AGAIN? ARE YOU NOT AWARE OF WHAT THE LAW SAYS?' Gal.4:8-11, 21**.

Believers, I want to assure you that Jesus did not leave us in a perplexed state before He ascended into heaven to continue interceding for us. Let's consider what He told us about this. Let us start with the animals and foods; Of course, it is true that Moses instructed the Israelites not to eat some kinds of animals, (Lev.11) but let us consider what Jesus said about this when it became a commandment. **"Again Jesus called the crowd to Him and said, listen to me, every one and understand this, nothing outside a man can make him unclean by going into him. Rather, it is what comes out of a man that makes him UNCLEAN. After He had left and entered the house, His disciples asked Him about this parable. Are you so dull? He asked, don't you see that nothing that enters a man from the outside can make him unclean? For it doesn't go into his heart but into his STOMACH, and then out of his body. IN SAYING THIS, JESUS DECLARED ALL FODDS CLEAN." Mark 7:14-19. (See Mark 7:6:23 for full details)**

Again, Jesus explained in another passage that they were forbidden to eat all foods and those laws were given to them because of their stubborn hearts. (See Matt.19:8). When Apostle Paul added his voice in support of Jesus' declaration that all foods are clean, he said; *"FOR EVERYTHING GOD CREATED IS GOOD, AND NOTHING IS TO BE REJECTED IF IT IS RECEIVED WITH THANKSGIVING, BECAUSE IT IS CONSECREATED BY THE WORD OF GOD AND PRAYER".* 1Tim.4:4-5.

When we consider these two statements by Jesus Christ and the Apostle Paul, we learn that we must not observe the law in our worshipping God in the New Testament service, because the law has been upgraded to a commandment. (See Matt.5:17-19, 22:34-40, Mark 12:28-31)

When the disciples started the church and the Gentiles were saved by God's grace and mercy, this upgraded law became a hot debate among them. They questioned whether the Gentiles must practice and worship God under the law. According to the scriptures, some of them who belonged to the party of the Pharisees, stood to their ground and said, '*the Gentile must be required to obey the law*'. (See the full story from Acts 15:1-35).

The apostles and elders met to make a decision about this problem which was among them. After much discussions, Peter got up and addressed them; **"Brothers, you know that sometimes ago God made a choice among you that the Gentiles might hear from my lip the message of the gospel and believe. God, who knows their hearts, showed that He accepted them by giving the Holy Spirit to them, just as He did to us. He made no distinction between us and them, for He purified their hearts by faith. NOW THEN, WHY DO YOU TRY TO TEST GOD BY PUTTING ON THE NECKS OF THE DISCIPLES A YOKE THAT NEITHER WE NOR OUR FATHERS HAVE BEEN ABLE TO BEAR? NO! WE BELIEVE IT IS THROUGH THE GRACE OF OUR LORD JESUS CHRIST THAT WE ARE SAVED JUST AS THEY ARE". Acts 15:5-11**.

We can see from the passage that Peter addressed them plainly that the Gentiles were not supposed to be oppressed by the law, since none of them nor their fathers were able to handle the terms of the law. He continued and warned them not to test God—meaning they should not to provoke God with this law which God gave to them because of their stubborn hearts. (Matt.19:8, Acts 15:10)

Again, the law was strictly given to them just to govern (control or guide) them on how to worship God. When Jesus met the Samaritan woman at the well, she brought that issue of how and where they had been strictly commanded to worship God. However, Jesus corrected her that it is no more necessary to choose a specific place, neither Jerusalem nor the mountain as was commanded before, but that worshipping God should be in SPIRIT AND IN TRUTH, for those who worship the Father in these two ways are doing the right thing in God's sight. (See John 4:19-24) Truly, Jesus did not abolish any of the law like it was perceived; instead He tried to simplify it for them. We can deduce from the dialogue between Jesus and the woman, that before their encounter anyone who wanted to worship God, had to travel to either the mountain or Jerusalem. However Jesus taught her that the true worshippers can now worship God in their home and even their own bed-rooms are equally approved for worshipping God. Is this not good?

Before Jesus came to the rescue of mankind, some of the law required the breaker or the offender to be stoned to death, but when the law became a commandment, the offenders are not to be punished directly by any human being. Now, everything is directly between individuals and God. Right now, it is God Himself who gives the punishment. If anyone commits any sin, it is a matter which has to be settled by the offender and his Father in heaven. No longer did the person who committed adultery face the penalty of death as it was before—this is what it called 'GRACE' and it was procured through the death of Jesus Christ. (See Col.2:13-15, 1:13-14)

Therefore, when Peter finished his speech, the whole assembly became silent as they listened to the accounts of Paul and Bannabas about the miraculous signs and wonders God had done among the Gentiles through them. Acts 15:12. When they finished, James finalized it and brought the debate to a successful conclusion when he even quoted from the Old Testament that the Gentiles must not be bothered with this Law which was given to them because of their stubborn hearts. (See Acts 15:13-21). He ended his speech that; *"IT IS MY JUDGEMENT THEREFORE, THAT WE SHOULD NOT MAKE IT DIFFICULT FOR THE GENTILES WHO ARE TURNING TO GOD. INSTEAD, WE SHOULD WRITE TO THEM TELLING THEM TO OBSTAIN FROM FOOD POLLUTED BY IDOLS, FROM SEXUAL IMMORALITY, FROM MEAT OF STRANGLED ANIMALS AND FROM BLOOD". Acts 15:19-20.*

After James' speech, all of them agreed and wrote a letter to the Gentiles that they do not a part of the law which God gave them through Moses, and so they were not to be burdened with it. (See Acts 151:-35) But note the conclusion part of the letter; "*THEREFORE, WE ARE SENDING JUDAS AND SILAS TO CONFIRM BY WORD OF MOUTH WHAT WE ARE WRITING. IT SEEMED GOOD TO THE HOLY SPIRIT AND TO US NOT TO BURDEN YOU WITH ANYTHING BEYOND THE FOLLOWING REQUIREMENTS; YOU ARE TO OBSTAIN FROM FOOD SACRIFICED TO IDOLS, FROM BLOOD, FROM THE MEAT*

OF SRTANGLED ANIMALS AND FROM SEXUAL IMMORALITY. YOU WILL DO WELL TO AVOID THESE THINGS. FAREWELL!" Acts 15:27-29.

After this incidence, the Apostle Paul who played a major role in it took advantage of it and elaborated on it to the Roman believers who were also confused about which foods they were allowed to eat and the ones which were forbidden. (Read Rom.14:1-23) But let's consider some verses to support this lesson; Rom.14:14, 20 says; *"As one who is in the Lord Jesus. I am fully convinced that 'NO' FOOD IS UNCLEAN IN ITSELF. BUT IF ANYONE REGARDS SOMETHING AS UNCLEAN, THEN FOR HIM IT IS UNCLEAN. DO NOT DESTROY THE WORK OF GOD FOR THE SAKE OF FOOD. ALL FOOD IS CLEAN".* This passage is an encouragement for those believers who do not know much about this subject, who are confused and have been carried away by false teachings. In this lesson, we have found out that Jesus declared all foods clean, (Mark 7:7-23) and the Apostle Paul also confirmed it. (Rom.14:10-21, 1Tim.4:4-5)

I hope the believers who read this book now know their stand in the Lord, and can enjoy any food they desire to eat without any condemnation, because there is 'NO' condemnation for those who are in Christ Jesus, because in Christ Jesus the LAW of the Spirit who gives life has SET YOU FREE from the law of sin and death. (Rom.8:1-2.)

This advice in the scriptures goes to the believers who still delight in worshipping God under the law and are confusing others with their wrong understanding of the scriptures about such a subject; "**I am confident in the Lord that you will take no other view. The one who is throwing you into confusion will pay the penalty, whoever he may be". Gal.5:10**. All believers must take careful note of this passage especially those who still believe and are teaching others that it is an abomination to eat certain kinds of foods and animals. The Apostle Paul wrote that we would pay the penalty if we caused anyone to fall from the faith because of what he eats. (See Rom. 14:10-15, 20)

Again, if you continue confusing others to go back to worshipping God under the law, which was extremely difficult for the Old Testament believers, (Acts 15:10) you will pay the penalty, no matter who you are and what you have done for the Lord in the ministry. This is because the death of Christ has redeemed us from under those harsh laws and we are no longer Gentiles but we have become heirs of God and co-heirs with Christ. Praise the Lord! (Read the following texts to refresh your memory on the subjects in order that no-one can take you captive for the law; Acts 15:10-11, Gal. 3:1-29, 4:1-31, 5:1-15, Rom.14:1-23.) But consider this passage; *"THEREFORE, DO NOT LET ANYONE JUDGE YOU BY WHAT YOU EAT OR DRINK, OR WITH REGARD TO A RELIGIOUS FESTIVAL, A NEW MOON CELEBRATION OR A SABBATH DAY. THESE ARE A SHADOW OF THE THINGS THAT WERE TO COME; THE REALITY, HOWEVER, IS FOUND IN CHRIST. DO NOT LET ANYONE WHO DELIGHTS IN FALSE HUMILITY AND THE WORSHIP OF ANGELS DISQUALIFY YOU. SUCH PEOPLE ALSO GO INTO GREAT DETAILS ABOUT WHAT THEY HAVE SEEN, (STUDIED AND KNOWN) AND THEIR UNSPIRITUAL MINDS PUFF THEM UP WITH IDLE NOTIONS. THEY HAVE LOST CONNECTION WITH THE HEAD, FROM WHOM THE WHOLE BODY, SUPPORTED AND HELD TOGETHER BY ITS LIGAMENTS AND SINEWS, GROWS AS GOD CAUSES IT TO GROW". Col.2:16-19.*

Believers! This is what the Bible tells you, in view of this, you should not worry at all of what you eat, because God has accepted you as a son by just believing in the Lord Jesus Christ who died for our sins and was raised for our justification. Therefore, you are free to eat any food or animal without condemnation. He condemns those who condemn and confuse you not to eat some kind of foods, animals and not to worship God on Sundays. See how He warns them; *"WHO ARE YOU TO JUDGE SOMEONE ELSE'S SERVANT? TO HIS OWN MASTER HE STANDS OR FALLS. AND HE WILL STAND, FOR THE LORD IS ABLE TO MAKE HIM STAND". Rom. 14:4.* What an interesting passage this is? Therefore, do not be confused about what food to eat, days to worship God and do not accept that you are breaking any law or commandments by doing so. We will do well to obey them, because Jesus did not abolish them, but He redeemed us from under it. (See Gal. 4:4-7, 5:10).

I hope this problem of the law has been solved, so now we can continue with our main subject—"the greatest and the second commandment". We have learned that Jesus did not abolish the law, but He redeemed us from under it and made it a commandment for us. On the other hand, if anyone thinks there is no more law and that God can be worshipped anyhow, that is a total deception. This is the deceitful way of the devil to entice us to break our fellowship with God. It gives him the chance to get us into his bondage. That is why some people claim to be Christians but they are being tormented by the devil. We thank God that we are aware of his devices. (John 10:10, 2Cor. 2:11)

I want to draw believers' attention to the fact that regardless of our identities and the churches we fellowship in, we must obey and practice this commandment to maintain our fellowship with God. These commandments were the law for the Israelites, and to my understanding, it has been upgraded to be the commandments for us. In the olden days, adultery attracted stoning to death and some other cruel punishments were given to offenders of the law by the people. In those days, if someone looked lustfully at a woman but had no sex with her, that was not a sin. When the law was upgraded and became a commandment, this act is as serious as the sin of sexual immorality. Jesus fulfilled this commandment by saying; "*You have heard that it was said, do not commit adultery. But I tell you that ANYONE WHO LOOKS AT A WOMAN LUSTFULLY HAS ALREADY COMMITTED ADULTERY WITH HER IN HIS HEART". Matt.5:27-28.* Can anybody claim Jesus abolished the law? No, instead, He fulfilled it, and divided all of them into two parts. The first part was named; 'The First and the greatest Commandment', and it comprises of the laws numbers one to number four. This first part of the commandment COMMANDS believers to show our love to God. The other part was also named as; 'The second commandment' and it comprises of the laws numbers five to ten. This part of the commandment also COMMANDS believers to show love to ourselves. (See Matt. 22:34-40)

Therefore, we are going to consider these ten laws and see if Jesus abolished, or fulfilled them. I hope after this lesson, we will know if some of us who worship on Sundays have thrown them away or not, as some unfortunate believers have already condemned us. They indicate that we are heading straight toward destruction, because their belief shows them we have thrown the commandments away.

(1) The law number one is; *"YOU SHALL HAVE NO OTHER GODS BEFORE ME". Exod.20:3.* Simply put, if we love God with all of our hearts, minds, souls, and strength, we will not worship any other gods nor seek help from them no matter what we are going through

in life. Truly, Jesus Christ did not abolish this law, it still stands firm. Believers are advised not to seek help from any other smaller gods, but we are to wait for the Almighty God alone to save us from any unwanted situation we find ourselves.

Are you in need of spouse, children, job, or any other thing? The Almighty God alone must be trusted and looked up to. If for any reason any believer seeks help from any other smaller gods, the law number one which falls within the first and greatest commandment has been broken. The difference between the law and the commandment is that whoever breaks the law receives instant punishment either directly from God or the people. But those who unintentionally break the commandment are not subject to any punishment.

"IF WE CONFESS OUR SINS, HE IS FAITHFUL AND JUST AND WILL FORGIVE US OUR SINS AND PURIFY US FROM ALL UNRIGHTEOUSNESS". 1John 1:9. "BLESSED ARE THOSE WHOSE TRANGRESSIONS ARE FORGIVEN, WHOSE SINS ARE COVERED. BLESSED ARE THOSE WHOSE SIN THE LORD DOES NOT COUNT AGAINST THEM AND IN WHOSE SPIRIT IS NO DECEIT". Psalm 32:1-2. We can see from this comparison that the commandment is better than the law, that is why Apostle Paul was very angry with the Galatians and asked them; *"HOW IS IT THAT YOU ARE TURNING BACK TO THOSE WEAK AND MESIRABLE PRINCIPLES? DO YOU WISH TO BE ENSLAVED BY THEM ALL OVER AGAIN?" Gal. 4:8-11, 21.*

(2) The law number two is; *"YOU SHALL NOT MAKE FOR YOURSELF ANY IDOL IN THE FORM OF ANYTHING IN HEAVEN ABOVE OR ON THE EARTH BENEATH OR IN THE WATERS BELOW. YOU SHALL NOT BOW DOWN TO THEM NOR WORSHIP THEM". Exod.20:4-6.* This is the law number two which Jesus did not abolish either. The disciples and the apostles neither broke nor abolished it and obviously, we are also obeying it because we love God with all of our HEARTS, MINDS SOULS AND STRENGTH.

Shadrach, Meshach and Abed-Nego REFUSED TO BOW DOWN and worship Nebuchadnezzar's golden image. They really loved God with all of their hearts, minds, souls and strength. (See Dan.3:1-30) Frankly speaking, Christians who worship on Sundays do not consider this law abolished. It is to be obeyed and Christians are not supposed to bow down to any image nor worship it no matter what the circumstances.

(3) The law number three is; *"YOU SHALL NOT MISUSE THE NAME OF THE LORD YOUR GOD, FOR THE LORD WILL NOT HOLD ANYONE GUILTLESS WHO MISUSES HIS NAME".* Exod.20:7. This is the third law which Jesus did not abolish instead He fulfilled it. See what He said about it; **"Again you have heard that it was said to the people a long ago, do not break your oath, but keep the oath you have made to the Lord. But I tell you, DO NOT SWEAR AT ALL; either by heaven, for it is God's throne; or by the earth, for it is His footstool; or by Jerusalem, for it is the city of the Great King. And do not SWEAR BY YOUR HEAD, for you cannot make even one hair white or black. SIMPLY LET YOUR 'YES' BE 'YES' AND YOUR 'NO' BE 'NO', ANYTHING BEYOND THIS COMES FROM THE EVIL ONE". Matt.5:33-37**.

This passage is a warning to those who misuse the name of the Lord frequently to indicate the truth of their case or story, such as,' I SWEAR TO GOD', I did not tell him this or that etc. Before Jesus fulfilled this law, believers were able to swear, but they had been warned not to use the name of the Lord in vain, as indicated in the passage we just read. However when Jesus was fulfilling it, He strictly commanded not to swear at all! No matter the doubt and disbelief of your challenger in any debate, do not swear at all even by the name of a human being, your own hair, a town, city or any other thing to indicate the truth of your story. Phrases like "I swear to you, I swear by my father, I swear by my mother, I swear by the steer in my hands" and so on are all not allowed in the New Testament worship. He said 'Let your 'Yes' be 'Yes' and your 'No' be 'No', if the truth is still being doubted in any circumstance, let the confused state remain and go your way in peace! Never say. 'I swear to God', 'I swear by my car' etc.

(4) The law number four is; *"REMEMBER THE SABBATH DAY BY KEEPING IT HOLY. SIX DAYS YOU HAVE LABOURED AND DO ALL YOUR WORK, THE SEVENTH DAY IS A SABBATH DAY TO THE LORD YOUR GOD. ON IT YOU SHALL NOT DO ANY WORK NEITHER YOU NOR YOUR SON NOR DAUGHTER NOR THE ALIEN WITHIN YOUR GATE. FOR SIX DAYS THE LORD MADE THE HEAVEN AND THE EARTH AND ALL*

> *THAT IS IN THEM, BUT HE RESTED ON THE SEVENTH DAY. THEREFORE, THE LORD BLESSED THE SABBATH DAY AND MADE IT HOLY". Exod.20:11.*

This law number four is particularly considered to be abolished by some believers. It is being assumed that believers who worship on any other day apart from Saturdays are not obeying this command. The simple answer is that there are some differences between the practices of the law and the commandment. Some of the laws are considered to be harsh, whereas the commandments are also considered to be harsh in some cases. For example, the practices of the laws numbers one and two are the same, because both the law and the commandment forbid believers to serve and seek help from any other smaller gods. But the commandment can be considered harder than the law in number three, because that law has some relief for believers, while the commandment is so strict. The law allowed believers to swear as long as the name of the Lord will not be used in vain, but the commandment does not allow any believer to swear at all! You see? Again, Jesus quoted in Matthew 5:27-28, which reads; **"You have heard that it was said, 'You shall not commit adultery'. But I tell you that anyone who looks at a woman lustfully has already committed adultery with her in his heart".** Do you see the difference between the law and the commandment in this passage? Of course, the law had some relief for us whereas the commandment is so strict on us.

On the contrary, the law was particularly given to guide the Israelites how to serve God because of their stubborn hearts. (Matt.19:8). Now, believers must be led by the Spirit of God to worship Him in Spirit and in truth, FOR THEY ARE THE KINDS OF WORSHIPPERS THE FATHER SEEKS, BUT NOT THOSE WHO OBSERVE THE LAW! (John 4:23-24, Rom.8:14) *"YOU ARE OBSERVING SPECIAL DAYS AND MONTHS AND SEASONS AND YEARS! I FEAR FOR YOU THAT SOMEHOW, I HAVE WASTED MY EFFORT ON YOU. TELL ME, YOU WHO WANT TO BE UNDER THE LAW, ARE YOU NOT AWARE OF WHAT THE LAW SAYS?" Gal.4:10, 11, 21.*

Apostle Paul kept reminding the New Testament believers that we are not worshipping God under the law, but we are to be led by the Spirit of God to worship Him in the Spirit through the commandment. For example, Jesus gave a command to His disciples to go into the whole world to proclaim the Good News to the people. Whoever believes, must be baptized in the name of the Father, the Son and the Holy Spirit, and must be taught to obey everything He has COMMANDED. (See Matt.28:19-20). This is not a law but a command! It is called; 'THE GREAT COMMISSION!' For this reason, I want to stress on this point that New Testament believers do not belong to the law, (See Acts 15:27-29), but we are being commanded to be led and guided by the Spirit to know the truth that sets free from all these complicated doctrines which is unfortunately studied with the wrong understanding by some believers. "*THEN YOU WILL KNOW THE TRUTH AND THE TRUTH WILL SET YOU FREE". John 8:32.*

On the other hand, I want to remind believers that the law was not completely abolished or thrown away by either Jesus or His disciples. The Ten Commandments which were the laws for the Israelites have something to do with us. We have already learnt that the law from number one to four deals with the love of believers towards God. For this reason, the Christian say they truly love God must do so with all of their heart, mind, soul and strength. It is imperative that such believers endeavor to honor God with a whole day specifically dedicated to worshipping Only Him without any diversion. (See Isaiah 58:13-14) Any day set aside for worship by your church authorities must be honored and kept holy to the Lord your God. Doing this is a sign of obedience to the Lord your God.

Sadly, some believers who worship only on Sundays have completely thrown away this law. The Scriptures below both confirm the need for us to honor the Sabbath day for the Lord our God if we really love Him and appreciate His divine sacrifice that has brought us peace and justification. *"IF YOU KEEP YOUR FEET FROM BREAKING THE SABBATH AND FROM DOING AS YOU PLEASE ON MY HOLY DAY, IF YOU CALL THE SABBATH A DELIGHT AND THE LORD'S HOLY DAY AND HONORABLE AND IF YOU HONOR IT BY NOT GOING YOUR OWN WAY AND NOT DOING AS YOU PLEASE OR SPEAKING IDLE WORD, THEN YOU WILL FIND JOY IN THE LORD AND I WILL CAUSE YOU TO RIDE ON THE HEIGHTS OF THE LAND AND TO FEAST ON THE INHERITANCE OF YOUR FATHER, JACOB. THE MOUTH OF THE LORD HAS SPOKEN". Isaiah 58:13-14.*

Christians should understand this passage clearly, because some Sunday worshippers think it is only Saturday worshippers who have been burdened to honor the Sabbath and keep it holy, it is a wrong notion and a misinterpretation of the word of God. According to the scriptures, Jesus did not abolish any of the laws, but after He had made them a commandment, He said. ALL THE LAW AND THE PROPHET HANG ON THESE TWO COMMANDMENTS. (See Matt.22:34-40.) Now, let's consider this; since all the laws are in this new commandment which we are advised to, why do we have to only exclude the fourth law? Always remind yourself that none of the laws are redundant or have been eliminated from the commandments, with this in mind, you will do well to keep the Sabbath day holy.

The second passage taken from the New Testament says; *"NOW WE WHO HAVE BELIEVED ENTER THAT REST, JUST AS GOD HAS SAID, THERE REMAINS THEN, A SABBATH-REST FOR THE PEOPLE OF GOD; FOR ANYONE WHO ENTERS GOD'S REST ALSO REST FROM HIS OWN WORK, JUST AS GOD DID FROM HIS. LET US THEREFORE MAKE EVERY EFFORT TO ENTER THAT REST, SO THAT NO-ONE WILL FALL BY FOLLOWING THEIR EXAMPLE OF DISOBEDIENCE". Heb.4:3, 9, 10, 11.* This is a powerful passage to tell you to rest and go to church for just one whole day throughout a week, because God Himself RESTED a whole day, how much more you, a mere man who is so occupied with various kinds of work or activities the whole week? The passage warns that you should make every effort to ENTER THAT REST the Bible is talking about and avoid emulating the examples of the disobedient believers. Therefore, keep the day set apart by your church leadership for worship, holy and honorable and the Lord will be pleased with you.

Now the Saturday worshippers will be glad to ask me then, if the Sabbath day is to be honored, why do some believers choose Sundays instead of Saturdays as the Sabbath? The answer to this question is also a question which looks like a warning from the Apostle Paul addressed to those who are so much concerned about the day they choose to honor as the Sabbath. He asked; *"WHO ARE YOU TO JUDGE SOMEONE ELSE'S SERVANT? TO HIS OWN MASTER, HE STANDS OR FALLS.* ***AND HE WILL STAND FOR THE LORD IS ABLE TO MAKE HIM STAND****. ONE MAN CONSIDERS ONE DAY MORE SACRED THAN ANOTHER. ANOTHER MAN CONSIDERS EVERYDAY ALIKE. EACH ONE SHOULD BE FULLY CONVINCED IN HIS OWN MIND". Rom.14:4-5.*

I hope this passage has enlightened you and erased any misconception or concerns you may have had about the day to be honored as holy and honorable to the Lord our God. This is because we should attempt to avoid going back to those weak and miserable principles, and wish to be enslaved by them all over again. (See Gal.4:8-11, 21)

Now to Sunday worshippers, this powerful Bible passage is encouraging you not to be worried about the day you choose to make it holy for the Lord your God. For he says; **'one man considers one day more sacred than another day, another also consider all days alike—no day is special than another'**. (Rom.4:4-5) Remember also that in the New Testament worship, A PLACE AND A DAY are not so important—what matters most is for you to keep the day you have faithfully and sincerely set apart to worship God, holy and honorable. (See John 4:19-24, Isaiah 58:13-14, Heb.4:3, 9-11)

Remember also that in the Acts of the Apostles chapter fifteen when a great argument arose about either the Gentiles should worship God in the same manner as the Jews; they all agreed that they should not be bothered with the Jewish custom and way of worship. (See Acts 15:1-35) The specific day we select to worship God is not important, what matters, is for us to WORSHIP THE FATHER IN SPIRIT AND IN TRUTH. This is the only way New Testament believers have been commanded to worship God. (See John 4:19-24)

Now to the believers who want to follow the Jewish method of keeping the Sabbath under the law, you should know that you are merely worrying yourselves, because you know how it expected to be observed, yet you are unable to do it exactly. In order for me to know the various views on the Sabbath, I have been a regular visitor to a variety of churches at different geographical locations both in—Ghana and in the USA. (I have therefore concluded that a number of Churches believe in and still want to worship God under the law—notably the Saturday churches.) On two occasions I was invited by my room-mates to visit a Saturday church service which I honored. According to the law, no-one is supposed to buy, sell or receive any money whatsoever from a business transaction. So for the members to obey this law accordingly, the church provides food for the congregation to eat after the service. But to my chagrin, in the course of the service, I noticed that a man secretly went out to buy bottles of water, covered them nicely and secretly shared them and I got one. The one who invited me is one of their elders, but he also got one. After the service, we went to where they dined. After dinner, I wanted a drink of water and when I was going out to buy some water to drink, he accompanied me and paid for two bottles of water for both of us.

Watch out for the interaction between a young girl and the Apostle Peter at the time Jesus was arrested. (See John 18:15-18, 25-27). A Similar case happened between my friend and one of the young girls in the church. This girl also came to the store to buy water with her friends but when she saw my friend paying for the water, she asked him why he was buying the water? To which he replied, “Oh it’s for my friend”. And her response was “but that is not right”! At that point, he remained silent, knowing very well that it was against their belief and he complained afterwards to me that the girl had attacked him. I asked him what was wrong with that and his reply was that it was wrong to buy or sell anything on the Sabbath day. When I inquired that “why did you then pay for it? He laugh and said, “One cannot do exactly what as the law says”. It was then that his wife added her voice and said, it is disobedience just like any other sin we normally commit. But why do you commit such an offence while you know it is a sin before God? I asked her. They laugh and the conversation was changed.

In fact, I do not know why some believers still want to worship God under the law, because according to the scriptures, by worshipping God under the law, no-one will be saved. According to the Apostle Peter’s description it is like ‘a yoke that neither their fathers nor themselves were able to bear’. *“NOW THEN, WHY DO YOU TRY TO TEST GOD BY PUTTING ON THE NECKS OF GENTILES A YOKE THAT NEITHER WE NOR OUR ANCESTORS HAVE BEEN ABLE TO BEAR?” Acts15:10.* The point I am putting across is that trying to worship God under the law cannot bring salvation, so let us welcome the Good News that Jesus died for our sins and was raised up for our justification. We have been made the children of God not of a husband’s will nor natural descent, but by the perfect will of God. (See John 1:11-13)

Through the death of Jesus Christ, we who once were far away have been brought near. (See Eph.2:1-13) If His death has saved us who were without hope and without God in the world (See Eph.2:12) Then we are glad to choose the DAY He rose from the death that brought us hope, justification and peace with God. For this reason, we are glad to choose that victorious DAY and make it holy and honorable even in more comparison with the day God RESTED! The rest that God had on Sabbath day could not save us; rather, it is the death and the resurrection of Jesus Christ that has saved us. We are therefore grateful for His resurrection and choose to worship Him on that VICTORIOUS DAY, make it holy and honorable.

We have found out that it is more important to honor the Sabbath and keep it holy, but not in the way those under the law observe it. It is better to observe it in the New Testament way which I hope you have now got enough information on it. If for any reason your job demands you to work on Saturday or Sunday, you are free to do so without any condemnation, because there is therefore no condemnation for those who are in Christ Jesus, through Christ Jesus, the law of the spirit of life sets us free from the law of sin and death. For what the law was powerless to do in that it was weakened by the sinful man to be a sin offering. And so He condemned sin in sinful man, in order that the righteous requirements of the law might be fully met in us, who do not live according to the sinful nature, but according to the Spirit. (See Rom.8:1-4)

I hope this biblical teaching will help you know what you must do as a child of God to maintain your fellowship with Him, all you have to do is to worship Him in spirit and in truth, for this is the type of worship the Father seeks. Therefore, believers who have accepted to worship God on that VICTORIOUS RESURRECTION DAY should advise themselves with these passages; **"I AM CONFIDENT IN THE LORD THAT YOU WILL TAKE NO OTHER VIEW. THE ONE WHO IS THROWING YOU INTO CONFUSION WILL PAY THE PENALTY WHO EVER HE MAY BE". Gal.5:10**. *"SEE TO IT THAT NO-ONE TAKES YOU CAPTIVE THROUGH HOLLOW AND DECEPTIVE PHILOSOPHY, WHICH DEPENDS ON HUMAN TRADITION AND THE BASIC PRINCIPLES OF THIS WORLD RATHER THAN IN CHRIST. HAVING BEEN BURIED WITH HIM IN BAPTISM AND RAISED WITH HIM THROUGH YOUR FAITH IN THE POWER OF GOD WHO RAISED HIM FROM THE DEAD". Col.2:8-12.*

We can see from the last passage that the baptism we received by immersion signifies that we also died and were buried with Christ and rose up with Him again on that victorious Sunday (that's the first day of the week, John

20:1). Now the question is; "If I died, rose up to a new life, became a new creature and I choose to worship the One who raised me up on that VERY DAY, the scriptures ask, what is wrong with it? No condemnation for those who choose to worship God on that victorious Sunday, make it holy and honorable. What matters is to REST and make it holy and your Lord will be pleased with you. (See Isaiah 58:13-14, Rom.14:1-23, Col.2:8-12).

Consider this passage to build your faith about this subject; *"THEREFORE DO NOT LET* ***ANYONE JUDGE YOU*** *BY WHAT YOU EAT OR DRINK, OR WITH REGARD TO A RELIGIOUS FESTIVAL, A NEW MOON CELEBRATION OR* ***A SABBATH DAY****. THESE ARE A SHADOW OF THE THINGS THAT WERE TO COME; THE REALITY, HOWEVER, IS FOUND IN CHRIST. DO NOT LET ANYONE WHO DELIGHTS IN FALSE HUMILITY AND THE WORSHIP OF ANGELS DISQUALIFY YOU. SUCH PEOPLE ALSO GO INTO GREAT DETAIL ABOUT WHAT THEY HAVE SEEN, AND THEIR UNSPIRITUAL MINDS PUFF THEM UP WITH IDLE NOTIONS. THEY HAVE LOST CONNECTION WITH THE HEAD, FROM WHOM THE WHOLE BODY, SUPPORTED AND HELD TOGETHER BY ITS LIGAMENTS AND SINEW, GROWS AS GOD CAUSES IT TO GROW". Col.2:16-19.*

This brings us to the end of part one of the law which is now the Greatest commandment. It comprises of the first through the fourth laws which commands us to demonstrate our love to God with all our hearts, minds, soul and with all our strength. The second commandment also comprises of the fifth up to the tenth laws which commands believers to show love to their neighbors. *"MAKE EVERY EFFORT TO LIVE IN PEACE WITH ALL MEN AND TO BE HOLY".* Heb.12:14.

The law which makes up this second commandment is as follows;

(5) Law number five is; "***HONOR YOUR FATHER AND MOTHER***". Exod. 20:12. Honor your father and mother does not mean to respect and love your parents alone, but it means to love and give respect to everyone either older or younger than you. Some people erroneously think that it is the children alone who have been commanded to respect and honor older people. We have been commanded to love ourselves—each other! (See John 17:20-26)

The Apostle Paul who carried the Gospel to the Gentiles, and also played a major role in deciding whether or not the Gentiles should obey the Law of Moses, has explained this issue clearly to us. (Acts 13:46-54, 15:12, Gal.2:14-21) Let us read what he wrote about this commandment and ascertain if it is the children alone who have been commanded to honor their parents; *"CHILDREN, OBEY YOUR PARENTS IN THE LORD FOR THIS IS RIGHT. HONOR YOUR FATHER AND MOTHER—WHICH IS THE FIRST COMMANDMENT WITH A PROMISE THAT IT MAY GO WELL WITH YOU AND THAT YOU MAY ENJOY LONG LIFE ON THE EARTH. FATHERS, DO NOT EXASPERATE YOUR CHILDREN; INSTEAD, BRING THEM UP IN THE TRAINING AND INSTRUCTION OF THE LORD. SLAVES, OBEY YOUR EARTHLY MASTERS WITH RESPECT AND FEAR, AND WITH SINCERE OF HEART, JUST AS YOU WOULD OBEY CHRIST. OBEY THEM NOT ONLY TO WIN THEIR FAVOR WHEN THEIR EYE IS ON YOU, BUT LIKE SLAVES OF CHRIST, DOING THE WILL OF GOD FROM YOUR HEART. SERVE WHOLE HEARTEDLY AS IF YOU WERE SERVING THE LORD NOT MEN, BECAUSE YOU KNOW THAT THE LORD WILL REWARD EVERYONE FOR WHATEVER GOOD HE DOES, WHETHER HE IS A SLAVE OR FREE. AND MASTERS, TREAT YOUR SLAVE IN THE SAME WAY. DO NOT THREATEN THEM, SINCE YOU KNOW THAT HE WHO IS BOTH THEIR MASTER AND YOURS IS IN HEAVEN AND THERE IS NO FAVORITISM WITH HIM". Eph.6:1-9.*

Let us take some lessons from the underlined words and sentences in the passage. The law demanded that children should honor their parents—(their fathers and mothers). But this time, that honor and obedience is first to go to their parents in the Lord! I hope you know that we have parents in the Lord? Parents in the Lord are our church's leaders which could be the deacons and deaconesses, elders, pastors and their wives, apostles and other high positions in the ministry. Again, these children here do not refer to our children at home—but it refers to the church members. This shows us that the members should do their best to honor and give due respect to the church officers which starts with the deacons and deaconesses to the highest hierarchy in the ministry. No matter how far you have been raised in life, either in education, financially, etc. you should still humble yourself before your church parents who are responsible for your spiritual welfare and the Lord will be pleased with you.

The next step is to honor your biological parents—this is the only aspect of the law that had the remarks, ‘this is the first commandment with the promise’. I hope we do not have a problem with this one, because it is the norm. If you are a child and you are reading this book, I want to reaffirm to you that you must do your best to honor and give the due respect to your parents and any older person around you, so that it may go on well with you in life.

The next instruction is; Fathers, do not exasperate your children, instead, bring them up in the training and instruction of the Lord. Let us start this from the fathers in the Lord who are our church leaders, either you are a presiding elder, a pastor or any of the position in the ministry of God. Just as you are expecting to be honored and respected, you are also being commanded to return this same honor and respect to your superiors, colleagues and church members.

Sometime ago, a group of church officers had a meeting with their district pastor. When an issue was brought to their attention to be discussed, they started sharing their views about the issue. Immediately one deaconess finished sharing her opinion, the pastor got angry and started insulting and rebuking her that, ‘you are my devil, you are a demon!’ Oh man of God! In actual fact, I was not at the meeting so I do not know exactly what the deaconess said, regardless, I think this man of God took things so far by the kind of utterances he made. I think this anointed man of God needed to refresh his mind with this Bible passage; *“GET RID OF ALL BITTERNESS, RAGE AND ANGER, BRAWLING AND SLANDER, ALONG WITH EVERY FORM OF MALICE. BE KIND AND COMPASSIONATE TO ONE ANOTHER, FORGIVING EACH OTHER, JUST AS IN CHRIST GOD FORGAVE YOU”. Eph.4:31-32.*

We as believers must NOT participate in any church activity and fight against ourselves, either orally or physically. No matter how bad people offend you, consider the above Bible passage and forgive them just as Christ also forgave you all your sins! This commandment demands that fathers in the Lord should NOT exasperate their children in the Lord. So after the pastor had addressed and insulted the deaconess as a demon, if she did not restrain herself and retaliated, could you imagine the chaos that would ensue from this provocation from that man of God? Again, the commandment demands that the fathers in the Lord should bring their children up in the TRAINING AND INTRUCTION OF THE LORD. What this means is that, even if the deaconess did not speak favorably of the pastor, he should have kindly corrected her in love but not in anger. Some believers who have encountered such humiliations could not withstand them and have found their way out of the church. Therefore, I want to plead to the Fathers in the Lord, please do your best to honor and respect your children in the Lord, for this is the promise that it may go well with the church and all the glory will be given to the Most High Jehovah God.

Now, fathers at home, please you too must try as much as possible to honor and respect your children without any exasperation, but bring them up in the GOOD TRAINING AND INTRUCTION OF THE LORD, and the Lord will be pleased with you and your home will be a happy home full of God's favor and glory with great achievement—say Amen!

The next is addressed to SLAVES who are to honor and respect their earthly masters with great love as if they are obeying and honoring Christ. Slaves here refer to the employees, students, maidservants and man servants (house-help or home caretakers), and you are commanded to honor and respect your earthly masters (Directors, managers and supervisors) with love and the Lord will be pleased with you.

Masters (Directors, Managers and supervisors) are not excluded from this commandment. They were free in the law, but in the commandment, they have a task to obey. The Bible passage can be understood that; 'Managers, masters, lecturers, professors, ministers and anyone in a top position, should threat their employees, students, maidservants, man servants and special assistants with love. Do not threaten them nor despise them because they are under you. If for any reason, all of us became bosses, who will serve us and what kind of order will we have in this world? However you threat your subordinates, you should be mindful of the fact that the One who is both their master and yours is watching you, because His eyes RANGE THROUGHOUT THE EARTH to see those whose hearts are fully committed to Him and to obey His commandment, they are believers who are always enjoy God's great fellowship. (See 2 Chron.16:9, Prov.1:33, Eph.6:9).

To sum it all up, we have learnt that nobody is to be excluded from this commandment which was law number five and it was for the children at home alone. But when it was fulfilled by Jesus and became the commandment, everyone on this earth has an obligation under this law. If you are not a child at home, you might be a father or mother. If you are not a child in the Lord (member), you might be a father or mother in the Lord (deacon or deaconess and upward positions). In your job, you may either be an employee, a supervisor or a manager and none of you are to be excluded from this commandment.

We can see from this lesson that Jesus did not abolish the law but He upheld (upgraded) it to be in full measures that everyone can worship God with LOVE because God Himself is love. (See 1John 4:8)

(6) Law number six is; "YOU SHALL NOT MURDER". Exod. 20:13. Recently, I had Bible discussion with a Bible school graduate who told me '**all thou shall not**' have been thrown away. Therefore, there is no condemnation for believers who sin. Any crime a believer commits does not count against him and he supported his belief with some Bible quotations, such as Isaiah 40:1-2, 54:8-9. According to his understanding, whatever sin a believer commits has automatically been forgiven. So are you telling me if I commit adultery, fornication, murderer, steal, or any other sin, I am free to do so? He said that, that is what the Bible says. Oh my God! So is this what you went to learn in the Bible school? Because of this knowledge, although he is a license minister of God as he claims, but he is living a questionable life. He has been trained to understand that once a person has been saved by God's grace, he is saved FOREVER! All his past and future sins have been forgiven and never to be remembered again, and so the life he leads does not count against him because he has been saved once and for all. When I tried to help him discover the proper meaning of the passages he had quoted, he got upset because he felt that he had graduated from a Bible College whereas I had not so I left him in that ignorant state of mind.

All I want believers to know is that the devil is very clever, so we must be aware of his devices, else he can use the same Bible which gives us knowledge about the word of God, to deceive and confuse us **to do what we ought not do as God's holy people.** (See 2Cor.2:11, Phil.2:12.)

In continuation, '**thou shall not murder**', is the sixth law which Jesus did not abolish, instead, He upheld it. Of course, all of thou shall not have been taken away, but were replaced with something meaningful. The place of thou shall not has not been left empty, that vacuum has been fully filled. Jesus did not create a vacuum in the scriptures that was left blank, hence he remarked that, all the law and the prophets hang on these two commandments. (See Matt. 22:34-40, Mark 12:28-31) For example, the Apostle Paul urged believers to put some nature and character to death and fill that place with something meaningful that will make the scriptures and believers complete. (See Gal.5:19-24, Col.3:5-10). Read the following passage; "*SINCE YOU HAVE TAKEN OFF YOUR **OLD SELF** WITH ITS PRACTICES, (THEN) PUT ON THE **NEW SELF**, WHICH IS BEING RENEWED IN KNOWLEDGE IN THE IMAGE OF ITS CREATOR". Col.3:9-10.* I hope you have already considered the underlined words, the old self was taken away, and the new self was put in its place. The slot of the old self was not left empty, but it was filled with some good words.

Again, the scriptures say, "*THEREFORE, IF ANYONE IS IN CHRIST, THE NEW CREATION HAS COME: THE **OLD** HAS GONE, THE **NEW** IS HERE". 2Cor.5:17.* (TNIV) I hope this passage will be meaningful to those who are giving these bad teachings to the people who are relying on them to supply them with some knowledge in the word of God. The **new creation** has come in place of the **old creation**.

What Jesus told us is that the law was not abolished but only the practices have changed, so let us read how He fulfilled law number six. The law required that believers should not murder, but He said; "*YOU HAVE HEARD THAT IT WAS SAID TO THE PEOPLE LONG AGO, 'DO NOT **MURDER**' AND ANYONE WHO MURDERS WILL BE SUBJECTED TO JUDGEMENT. BUT I TELL YOU THAT ANYONE WHO IS ANGRY WITH HIS BROTHER WILL BE SUBJECTED TO JUDGEMENT. AGAIN, ANYONE WHO SAYS TO HIS BROTHER, 'RACA' IS ANSWERED TO THE SANHEDRIN. BUT ANYONE WHO SAYS; 'YOU FOOL' WILL BE IN DANGER OF THE FIRE OF HELL". Matt.5:21-26.* Dear readers, is the law abolished? Definitely NOT! The way I have stated the passage with the underlined words proves that Jesus did not completely eradicate it, instead He fulfilled it.

When the Apostle Paul was also strengthening this law, he said; "AND THE SERVANT OF THE LORD MUST NOT QUARREL, INSTEAD, HE MUST BE KIND TO EVERBODY. THOSE WHO OPPOSE HIM MUST BE GENTLY INTRUCTED IN THE HOPE THAT GOD WILL GRANT THEM REPENTANCE LEADING TO A KNOWLEDGE OF TRUTH, AND THAT THEY WILL COME TO THEIR SENSES AND ESCAPE FROM THE TRAP OF THE DEVIL, WHO HAS TAKEN THEM CAPTIVE TO DO HIS WILL". 2Tim.2:24-26. So far I hope you have understood that the law did not only instruct that believers should not murder but also that they should not even engage in a quarrel or fight.

Jesus concluded and said; *"IF YOU ARE GOING TO GIVE YOUR OFFERING AND THERE REMEMBER THAT YOUR BROTHER HAS SOMETHING AGAINST YOU; LEAVE YOUR GIFT THERE IN FRONT OF THE ALTER. FIRST GO AND RECONCILE TO YOUR BROTHER, THEN COME AND OFFER YOUR GIFT". Matt.5:23-24.* I am sure this passage does not show any sign that Jesus abolished the law, but He said, 'all the laws hang on these two commandments. Therefore, believers who are not in good terms with others should be very careful and advise themselves with this lesson. I always try to remind believers that people who were at the back of the gate of the kingdom of God in Jesus' illustration, (Matt.7:21-23, Luke 13:22-31) they were not pagans or unbelievers, but they were believers who could not understand the word of God properly and for that reason practiced it wrongly. Pagans and unbelievers have already been condemned so they have no case to challenge, but believers who got the message from false teachers and practiced it in a wrong way, are those who find it hard to believe that after all their efforts to serve God, they are denied access into that beautiful City (HEAVEN). Therefore, be advised!

(7) Law number seven is; "YOU SHALL NOT COMMIT ADULTERY". Exod. 20:14. When Jesus was fulfilling this law He said; *"YOU HAVE HEARD THAT IT WAS SAID; DO NOT COMMIT ADULTERY. BUT I TELL YOU THAT ANYONE WHO LOOKS AT A WOMAN LUSTFULLY HAS ALREADY COMMITTED ADULTERY WITH HER IN HIS HEART". Matt.5:27-28.*

This statement made by Jesus shows that he truly fulfilled the law, because the old testament believers were free to look at a woman lustfully and go their way without any consequences, but this is not so in our dispensation. The time has come that the true worshippers, worship the Father in spirit and in truth. Now, the Spirit of the living God has made His dwelling in our hearts, hence, we must keep our body completely pure for Him to feel comfortable within us, (**See 1Cor.6:19-20, Gal.4:30**), that is why the law has been upgraded to this far. We can safely say that if anyone loves his brother/neighbor, he will not sleep with his wife or daughter. Consequently, if anyone claims to be a child of God and he disobeys this command, he is deceiving himself and can be described as a 'PROFFESSED CHRISTIAN'.

(8) The eighth law is; "YOU SHALL NOT STEAL". Exod. 20:15. I hope nobody has misconstrued that this law was abolished by Jesus. It is still a command which every believer is expected to obey, because if you love your neighbor/brother, you will not take anything that belongs to him without his consent. Those who take guns and other weapons to attack people and rob them do not have any love or regard for their neighbors. On the other hand, some believers may not rob their neighbors with weapons, but are not excluded from stealing at homes, market, offices and other places and even at church. The church funds could be stolen by those who are in-charge of it. If you are a believer who still has this habit of stealing, you should make every effort to put an end to it before it leads you into disgrace.

(9) Law number nine is; **"YOU SHALL NOT GIVE FALSE TESTIMONY AGAINST YOUR NEIGHBOR". Exod. 20:16**. This law also has not been abolished by Jesus, so whenever the need arises for you to testify about anyone or to give an eye witness' account of an incident, please ensure that you give an accurate description of events and the Lord will be pleased with you.

Pastors, elders, deacons and deaconesses should be very careful when they are giving testimonies about the characters and conducts of the various ministers who are being transferred to other stations. These testimonies must be true and concise, because standing in the presence of God to give a false testimony to please people is very dangerous. If for any reason you cannot include their weaknesses, I suggest that you just say the good aspects of their deeds that you know and leave it at that, rather than adding things which are not true just to praise or please them.

Once, a farewell church service was being held for a district pastor who was being transferred from his district to another. The presiding elder who was chosen to give a testimony about the pastor said something which was not true so the entire congregation started murmuring and there was such a chaos in the temple. You see! All the members had been with the pastor for the past four years, so they also knew him, but the elder tried to give a testimony that would cover his weaknesses before the congregation and especially the strangers. This commandment stresses that believers should not to give a false testimony or witness against their neighbors, neither to harm, disgrace, help, nor to please them.

(10) The tenth law is; "YOU SHALL NOT COVET YOUR NEIGHBOR'S HOUSE. YOU SHALL NOT COVET YOUR NEIGHBORS'S WIFE, OR HIS MANSERVANT OR MAIDSERVANT, HIS OX OR DONKEY, OR ANYTHING THAT BELONGS TO YOUR NEIGHBOR". Exod. 20:17. I hope this passage is very clear to every believer's understanding, because if you love your neighbor you will not be jealous of his beautiful wife, children, house, cars, dog, ox, cattle and anything that belongs to him. If your neighbor's wife is quite beautiful than yours, instead of coveting and criticizing her, you will do well to praise God for him. If you love your neighbor and he receives God's blessings, and a great success comes his way, you will not accuse him of possessing dirty money while you know for a fact that he is not involved in any dirty business. Again if your neighbor gets a prompt promotion, you should not be covetous and complain that it was you who deserved it. You may be in the ministry of God for so long and yet a novice may be promoted to a higher position than you, the word of God under this commandment instructs that you should not covet his position and the Lord will be pleased with you.

In conclusion, this is the law the Lord gave to His people through Moses, Jesus Christ did not abolish or erase it. The disciples and the apostles did not eradicate it neither did the believers who worshiped God on that VICTORIOUS RESURRECTED SUNDAY. It stands therefore to say that anyone who thinks Sunday worshippers are destroying it and should be condemned is conceited and has got the message all wrong. (1Tim.6:3-5). We can see from this lesson that none of the laws has been thrown away, therefore I encourage and urge everyone who wants to maintain his fellowship with God, to properly obey them in order to continue to enjoy being in the kindness of God. Do not forget that my aim of writing this book is to EXPOSE the devil's tricks and traps to believers. He knows since we have been ENGRAVED IN THE PALM of God, (See Isaiah 49:14-17, Jer.20:11, Psalm 31:20, Rom.8:31, Heb.13:6,) it is impossible for him to reach us and succeed in his evil's plans against us. (Read this Bible passage to see what the devil is doing against you without your knowledge. **PSALM 37:12-15**) When you find out what the devil is planning against you, it will help you take this lesson seriously in order for you to maintain your fellowship with God by obeying His COMMANDMENTS. I hope you have not forgotten this Bible passage; **"IF YOU LOVE ME, YOU WILL OBEY MY COMMANDMENT" John 14:15**.

CHAPTER 5

THE OLD AND NEW COMMAND

The old command refers to the second commandment which Jesus taught believers to love one another; '**Love your neighbor as yourself**'. (Matt.22:34-40) It is the law the Lord gave to His people through Moses, Jesus fulfilled and divided it into two parts as we have just learnt in chapter four of this book. We found out that the second part of the law commands believers to show love to each other, and this is what John kept emphasizing to believers and he rewrote it again with much more details and named it; 'THE NEW COMMAND'. Here, John wanted to remind believers that what he was writing is not a different command, but an 'OLD ONE', which he renamed; 'NEW COMMAND'. This is how he wrote it; *"DEAR FRIENDS, I AM NOT WRITING YOU A NEW COMMAND BUT AN OLD ONE WHICH YOU HAVE HAD SINCE THE BEGINNING. THE OLD COMMAND IS THE MESSAGE YOU HAVE HEARD—WHOEVER LOVES HIS BROTHER LIVES IN THE LIGHT AND THERE IS NOTHING IN HIM TO MAKE HIM STUMBLE. THE OLD COMMAND IS SEEN IN HIM AND YOU, BECAUSE THE DARKNESS IS PASSING AND THE TRUE LIGHT IS ALREADY SHINNING. ANYONE WHO CLAIMS TO BE IN THE LIGHT, BUT HATE HIS BROTHER IS STILL IN DARKNESS AND WALKS AROUND IN THE DARKNESS; HE DOES NOT KNOW WHERE HE IS GOING, BECAUSE HE HAS BEEN BLINDED BY THE DARKNESS". 1John 2:7-11.*

Jesus Christ could not get enough time to explain His teachings and He left that work to the Holy Spirit to continue from where He ended. The Holy Spirit is to explain and teach us in much more details for easier understanding of the word of God. *"BUT THE COUNCELOR, THE HOLY SPIRIT, WHOM THE FATHER WILL SEND IN MY NAME, WILL TEACH YOU ALL THINGS, AND WILL REMIND YOU OF EVERYTHING I HAVE SAID TO YOU". John 14:26.*

Thus, John understood this and was able to explain it clearly to us through the inspiration of the Holy Spirit. He simplified this second commandment in his first epistle. Please read 1John 3:10-24 to see how he explained it. But check this passage; "*THIS IS HOW WE KNOW WHO THE CHILDREN OF GOD (CHRISTIANS) ARE AND WHO ARE THE CHILDREN OF THE DEVIL (UNBELIEVERS). ANYONE WHO DOES NOT DO WHAT IS RIGHT IS NOT A CHILD OF GOD, NOR IS ANYONE WHO DOES NOT LOVE HIS BROTHER. THIS IS THE MESSAGE YOU HEARD FROM THE BEGINNING, WE SHOULD LOVE ONE ANOTHER*". 1 John 3:10-11. This passage needs to be used for self-judgment or examination by Christians, because it reveals those who are truly the children of God and those who are the children of the devil. 'A word to the wise is enough!' Believers, let us examine ourselves with this passage and see if belong to God or to the devil.

Again read this passage to know if you are a child of God or not. "WE KNOW THAT WE HAVE PASSED FROM DEATH TO LIFE BECAUSE WE LOVE OUR BROTHERS. ANYONE WHO DOES NOT LOVE HIS BROTHER REMAINS IN DEATH. ANYONE WHO HATES HIS BROTHER IS A MURDERER, AND YOU KNOW THAT 'NO' MURDERER HAS ETERNAL LIFE IN HIM". 1 John 3:14-15. I can see that John did not want us as believers to deceive ourselves with the name of the Lord that we are the children of God, but he was addressing those who have the 'ASSURANCE OF SALVATION'. Because he had earlier recorded in the gospel that; 'Anyone who believes in the Son has eternal life'. (John 3:16, 36.) This gospel implies that although you may already have assurance of salvation, because you believe in Jesus and in your church you may either be a member, elder, deacon, deaconess or a pastor or any other high office in the ministry, but he is speaking from the inspiration of the Holy Spirit to tell us that failing or refusing to

SHOW LOVE to your brother or neighbor proves that you are not a child of God and you have 'NO' LIFE in you.

In addition a person is seen as a 'MURDERER' if he fails or refuses to love his brother. I am sure he did not want us to be misled by his gospel message that is why he clearly explained the status of believers in this epistle. All he was saying was confirming what Jesus Himself said which recorded in John 14:15, "IF YOU LOVE ME OBEY MY COMMANDMENT". He clearly understood what Jesus meant, that if He is the One you have accepted, then obey His commandment. So we can see obeying the commandment will determine who has really believed in Him. Dear reader, are you sure you believe in Jesus Christ as your Lord and personal savior? Then obey His commandment and love your brother as yourself, and this will give you the assurance of salvation.

A while back, a church member and his wife came to me for financial assistance. After they narrated their story, I wondered why that man was in such a huge financial constraint, because I knew his older brother was very rich and well known in the country. In fact, his rich brother often led the offertory and gave the highest contributions in support of the kingdom's business; as a result he commanded great respect at church. Therefore, he was capable of supplying all his brother's needs. This man started crying like a baby when I asked him about his wealthy brother. This is a very sad story indeed! What are we doing as believers? Are we taking the word of God for a joke? Do you love your brother? What do you do to show that you love your brother? Anyway, without the highest desire to brag about how I have had the privilege to be kind, I was able to help them in their time of needs. But I want believers to be reminded that salvation is received free of charge, but since we are not yet dead and the coming of the Lord is not yet upon us, we are advised to work hard until Christ comes to see us as people who have faithfully served Him and obeyed His commandments. Otherwise, we will be surprised at His coming, because He has made it known to us that, he who stands firm or faithfully to the end will be saved. (Matt.10:22).

Therefore, I am reminding believers through this book that Satan knows all these principles so he is always looking for a way to entice believers to be recalcitrant due to our lack of knowledge (See Hosea 4:6, Prov.4:16, 2 Cor.2:11) The devil knows that these bad attitudes bring God's discipline to believers who allow the devil to lure them to do the things which are contrary to His commandment. However, this is the perfect will of the devil so that he can also take advantage of the disobedient believers.

Consequently, I want all believers who really cherish their salvation to take the lessons in this book seriously and allow the Holy Spirit to give you a deeper insight into the word of God. As a sign of dissatisfaction with the lifestyle of some believers, Jesus openly said; **"WHY DO YOU CALL ME LORD! LORD! AND YOU DO NOT DO WHAT I SAY?" Luke 6:46**. And John also continued; "*FOR ANYONE WHO DOES NOT LOVE HIS BROTHER WHOM HE HAS SEEN, CANNOT LOVE GOD WHOM HE HAS NOT SEEN. AND HE HAS GIVEN THIS COMMAND; WHOEVER LOVES GOD MUST ALSO LOVES HIS BROTHER*". 1 John 4:20-21.

The whole chapter four of first John talks about this command that believers should love their brothers, read these verses; *"DEAR FRIENDS, LET US LOVE ONE ANOTHER, FOR LOVE COMES FROM GOD. EVERY ONE WHO LOVES HAS BEEN BORN OF GOD AND KNOWS GOD. WHOEVER DOES NOT LOVE DOES NOT KNOW GOD BECAUSE GOD IS LOVE. NO-ONE HAS EVER SEEN GOD, BUT IF WE LOVE ONE ANOTHER, GOD LIVES IN US AND HIS LOVE IS MADE COMPLETE. AND SO WE KNOW AND RELY ON THE LOVE GOD HAS FOR US.* ***GOD IS LOVE. WHOEVER LIVES IN LOVE LIVES IN GOD, AND GOD LIVES IN HIM****. IN THIS WAY, LOVE IS MADE COMPLETE AMONG US SO THAT WE WILL HAVE* ***CONFIDENCE ON THE DAY OF JUDGMENT****, BECAUSE IN THIS WORLD WE ARE LIKE HIM". 1John 4:7, 8, 12, 16, 17.*

The underlined words in the above passage must be clearly understood. It says that the LOVE we have been commanded to show to our brothers, that LOVE IS GOD! Thus, any believer who LIVES IN LOVE, (since God LOVE), he lives in God and God also lives in him, and that makes him a COMPLETE CHRISTIAN who has the full assurance of salvation.

Now consider this question; Why does this believer have the assurance of salvation? This is because the LOVE which is reigning in him is God and no-one will carry God into the fire of hell which is the final destination for those who cannot make it to heaven. This is the reason why Jesus spent some time praying for His disciples and all believers to LOVE themselves (John 17:6-26). This is to ensure that we do not waste our time, money, strength and other resources to serve God and still find ourselves in an unwanted and unexpected fire of hell. (Matt.5:22). I hope you have got some good points from this chapter, so let us see what the next chapter has for us, but before we tackle the next chapter, kindly read these Bible passages for more details. 1John 3:10-18, 4:1-end.

CHAPTER 6

LOVE IN ACTION

I have clearly elaborated to you the love Christians should have for their brothers and others. In this chapter, we are going to learn what this LOVE is. What do you do to show that you LOVE your brother or someone? Again, how do we know God loves us? *"DEAR FRIENDS, SINCE GOD LOVES US, WE ALSO OUGHT TO LOVE ONE ANOTHER".* 1 John 4:11. This passage challenges believers that since God loves us, we must also love one another, because this will give us CONFIDENCE AND HOPE that we are His children and our salvation is assured for the judgment day. (1 John 4:17)

It is a sad story for some believers to claim to have accepted Jesus Christ as their Lord and personal Savior, still they do not have the assurance of salvation. This is because though they have openly confessed their faith and frequently attend church service, yet they might not obey this command of God which gives and provides the assurance of salvation to believers who have faithfully accepted Him. **(John 14:15, 1John 5:1-12).** *"THIS IS HOW WE KNOW THAT WE LOVE THE CHILDREN OF GOD:* ***BY LOVING GOD AND CARRYING OUT HIS COMMANDS.*** *AND HIS COMMANDS ARE NOT BURDENSOME. FOR EVERYONE BORN OF GOD OVERCOMES THE WORLD. THIS IS THE VICTORY THAT HAS OVERCOME THE WORLD, EVEN OUR FAITH".* 1 John 5:2-4. According to the passage, openly confessing your faith, attending church services and holding some positions do not qualify you to be a child of God or to be saved on the judgment day without having the love to obey His commands.

Again, some believers also think that they are saved because of how they understand the salvation process. But in this lesson we are discovering the mystery of who is supposed to have the confidence of being saved on the judgment day? The person who can lay claim to salvation on the judgment day is the **one who has God in him.** And the lesson has revealed that the God who is supposed to be in us is LOVE! "**FOR GOD IS LOVE**". 1John 4:8. Therefore, whoever loves has God in him and is in God and this gives him complete hope to be saved when His glory is revealed.

Now, the question is, how can we know we have love in us? What shows that there is love in you? In other words, what do you do to show that you love your brother or anyone? Before we search for the answer to these questions, first let us find out how God demonstrated His love for us, as an example of what shows you love someone, and what love really is. *"THIS IS HOW GOD SHOWED HIS LOVE AMONG US; HE SENT HIS ONE AND ONLY SON INTO THE WORLD THAT WE MIGHT LIVE THROUGH HIM.* ***THIS IS LOVE,*** *NOT THAT WE LOVED GOD, BUT THAT HE LOVED US AND SENT HIS SON AS ATONING SACRIFICE FOR OUR SIN".* **Praise The Lord! 1 John 4:9-10.**

The above passage has explained in detail how God showed His love for us. He did not only show His love for us by word of mouth only, pronouncements—but in **ACTION**! He ACTED and sent His Only begotten Son to save us from death, destruction, the power of the devil and to provide ETERNAL LIFE to all who believe in Him. We, who were once far away have been brought near and saved through the blood of His Only Son Jesus Christ, (Eph.2:1-13). This is how we know that God has loved us and He wants us also to show love to each other in **ACTION**, not just by mere utterances; **"I LOVE YOU"**

At this point, we are going to study how to express our love to our brothers/neighbors? *"THIS IS HOW WE KNOW WHAT LOVE IS; **(He is explaining what the love we are talking so much about really is, so pay close attention to the full explanation.)** JESUS CHRIST LAID DOWN HIS LIFE FOR US. AND WE OUGHT TO LAY DOWN OUR LIVES FOR OUR BROTHERS. IF ANYONE HAS MATERIAL POSSESSIONS AND SEES HIS BROTHER IN NEED BUT HAS NO PITY ON HIM, HOW CAN THE LOVE OF GOD BE IN HIM? DEAR CHILDREN, LET US NOT LOVE WITH WORDS OR TONGUES BUT WITH ACTION*

AND IN TRUTH". 1 John 3:16-18. This passage answers all the questions we have been tackling from chapter five to this very chapter about the love believers have been commanded to show to one another. It is not supposed to be a camouflaged love—sweet words, but in ACTION! Just as God acted on His love for mankind by giving us the greatest gift of all (His Son Jesus Christ), we have also been commanded to emulate that love—ACTION! (See 1 John 3:16-18, 4:9-11.)

Although, we cannot literally die to save our brothers, but what is expected of us is to assist the needy people among us with our material resources such as clothes, shirts, shoes, money, accommodation, cars, jobs or any other thing that can make someone live happily in Christ Jesus. Do you know that we have some believers in our midst who are not comfortable in life because they lack the above mentioned things? The love we have been commanded to exhibit to our brothers also includes providing mental, physical and emotional help to those in distress. If anyone lacks any of these things and you who are in a position to assist them refuse to do so, God questions you; how can you say you love your brother and obey His commands? (See 1 John 3:16-24).

All that I am trying to draw believers' attention to in this lesson is that anyone who claims to be a child of God or Christian, but fails or refuses to show 'Love in Action' to the needy among us proves Him wrong! Because the children of God obey their Father's commands and show love in action to their brothers in needs.

To support all numerous passages in this subject, I'm writing the next passage to help you understand it better, in case you have 'no' Bible with you to read the references we have provided. "*THIS IS HOW WE BELONG TO THE TRUTH AND HOW WE SET OUR HEARTS AT REST IN HIS PRESENCE. IF OUR HEARTS COMDEMNS US, WE KNOW THAT GOD IS GREATER THAN OUR HEARTS AND HE KNOWS EVERYTHING.* ***(It means, if you have sincerely and faithfully believed in Him, He knows, because nothing is hidden from Him. He knows and discerns it from our hearts-let us continue)*** *DEAR FRIENDS, IF OUR HEARTS DO NOT CONDEMN US, WE HAVE CONFIDENCE BEFORE GOD AND RECEIVE FROM HIM ANYTHING WE ASK,* ***BECAUSE WE KEEP HIS COMMANDS AND DO WHAT PLEASES HIM.*** *AND THIS IS HIS COMMAND: TO BELIEVE IN THE NAME*

OF HIS SON, JESUS CHRIST, <u>AND TO LOVE ONE ANOTHER AS HE COMMANDED US</u>. THOSE WHO KEEP HIS COMMANDS LIVE IN HIM, AND HE IN THEM. AND THIS IS HOW WE KNOW THAT HE LIVES IN US: WE KNOW IT BY THE SPIRIT HE GAVE US". 1 John 3:19-24.

This particular passage shows us the process we need to go through to become Christians—children of God. The first sentence says; 'this is how we know we belong to the truth and set our hearts at **REST** in His presence—this means, you have confidence to be saved because you belong to God, this is; **"THE ASSURANCE OF SALVATION".** Then it continues to explain what you must do to attain that assurance of salvation. The first step is; **to believe in His Son Jesus Christ,** and the next is, **to obey His command by showing 'LOVE IN ACTION' to one another—to the needy among us**. When anyone positions himself in this way, he needs no-one else to tell him he is saves, but he himself can have that inner conviction.

Sometimes, some ministers of God accuse others that they are the cause of their members not having the 'ASSURANCE OF SALVATION' and still live in confusion. As a matter of fact, this cannot be true, because according to the passage, when one qualifies to be saved, he may know this by the Spirit God gave him. Once you believe in Him and keep His commandment, you live in Him and He also lives in you, and the moment He lives in you, you are saved at that particular time. I said it before that no-one will carry God into condemnation—hell! You can read from 1John 3:16-24 to buttress this point.

Sometimes ago, a certain man set a good example of this '**<u>Love in Action</u>**' at the church service. This man asked the church secretary to announce that anyone who is in debt should see him immediately after the service. According to him, he had been commanded by the Holy Spirit to pay off the debts of the members of the congregation so that they would stop thinking about it and enjoy the presence of the Lord. It was not a joke; there was a long queue by the members who needed money to settle their debts. Truly, this man honored his word and gave out sufficient money that could settle all their debts. Hallelujah! This is called 'Love in Action' because he ACTED in Love!

Believers, have any of you done anything of such a nature to express your love to such an extent as a sign of your obedience to this command? If your answer is 'Yes' then may God bless you and continue doing good because God has stored many good promises for all who obey this command and show this kind of love to their brothers in need. Read some of the promises; *"CAST YOUR BREAD UPON THE WATERS, FOR AFTER MANY DAYS YOU WILL FIND IT AGAIN. GIVE PORTIONS TO SEVEN, YES TO EIGHT, FOR YOU DO NOT KNOW WHAT DISASTER MAY COME UPON THE LAND". Eccl.11:1-2.* **"ONE MAN GIVES FREELY, YET GAINS EVEN MORE; ANOTHER WITHHOLDS UNDULY, BUT COMES TO POVERTY. A GENEROUS MAN WILL PROSPER; HE WHO REFRESHES OTHERS WILL HIMSELF BE REFRESHED".** Prov.11:24-25. Now take a look at this passage carefully, for it has a bountiful meaning; **"HE WHO IS KIND TO THE POOR LENDS TO THE LORD AND HE WILL REWARD HIM FOR WHAT HE HAS DONE". Prov.19:17.**

The reason the Lord has commanded us to show love to one another especially to the needy among us is because when a poor man cries and prays to God, He will not send money from heaven to him just as He sent manna from heaven for the Israelites on the desert. **God expects those already blessed to help these poor and needy ones among us**. *"LET US NOT BECOME WEARY IN DOING GOOD, FOR AT THE PROPER TIME WE WILL REAP A HARVEST IF WE DO NOT GIVE UP. THEREFORE, AS WE HAVE OPPORTUNITY, LET US DO GOOD TO ALL PEOPLE ESPECIALLY TO THOSE WHO BELONG TO THE FAMILY OF BELIEVERS". Gal.6:9-10.*

According to this passage, we can see that God uses His own people to bless His own. That is why He said, 'He who is kind to the poor lends to the Lord who as a result will reward him for that kindness'. Prov.19:17. This passage shows that what that philanthropist did when he gave out huge amounts of money to settle the debts of the church members, will be richly rewarded because that money was lent to God and He will repay him a double fold, and I am very sure this man will never be in need of anything as long as God lives and reigns. This is 'Love in Action!' Because God ACTED and sent His only Son to save mankind from the devil's bondage. (Eph.2:1-13, 1Peter 1:18-21, 1John 3:16-24.) And this philanthropist also

ACTED and gave out huge amount of money to pay the debts of the people he may not know personally. What about you? What have you done to show you have participated in this kind of love which believers have been commanded to do as children of God? (1John 3:1-24, 4:7-11, 5:2-4) This is a rhetorical question. The next chapter also has something else for you.

CHAPTER 7

A SINCERE LOVE

*"NOW THAT YOU HAVE PURIFIED YOURSELF BY **OBEYING** THE TRUTH SO THAT YOU HAVE **SINCERE LOVE** FOR YOUR BROTHER, **LOVE ONE ANOTHER DEEPLY**, FROM THE HEART". 1 Peter 1:22.* This kind of love is very real, has no deception to it, it is not a lie, but it is a true and real love being shown one to another. Some people take advantage of their wealth to despise and mock the needy or poor people among us when they go to them for financial assistance. Instead of these rich people telling them upfront that they cannot assist them, they deceive them with a lot of appointments, and many more excuses. They keep deceiving them, until the one in need himself realizes he is being despised and ridiculed before he ceases going to them with any request.

If you are one of these people who like to deceive people who are really in need, then, I advise you never to do that again, else, one day you will MEET God's WRATH. You may not know who that person really is. Any of them could be directed by God through prayers to come to you for assistance, and if you deceive them God will not be happy about it. Check these passages carefully; *"HE WHO IS KIND TO THE POOR LENDS TO GOD, AND HE WILL REWARD HIM FOR WHAT HE HAS DONER". Prov.19:17.* The opposite of this passage is; 'HE WHO DECEIVE THE POOR DECEIVE GOD, AND HE WILL REWARD OR REPAY HIM FOR WHAT HE HAS DONE TO THAT POOR MAN' = (IS EQUAL TO) *"DO NOT BE DECEIVED, **GOD CANNOT BE MOCKED**. A MAN REAPS WHAT HE SOWS. THE ONE WHO SOWS TO PLEASE SINFUL NATURE, FROM THAT NATURE WILL*

REAP DESTRUCTION*; THE ONE WHO SOWS TO PLEASE THE SPIRIT, FROM THE SPIRIT WILL REAP ETERNAL LIFE. LET US NOT BECOME WEARY IN DOING GOOD, FOR AT THE PROPER TIME WE WILL REAP A HARVEST IF WE DO NOT GIVE UP.* ***THEREFORE, AS WE HAVE THE OPPORTUNITY, LET US DO GOOD TO ALL PEOPLE ESPECIALLY TO THOSE WHO BELONG TO THE FAMILY OF BELIEVERS****". Gal.6:7-10.*

My dear reader if you happen to be one of those who do such things to people in need, please think about these passages and their meaning, I urge you to pray for forgiveness if you have done this in the past and never do it again, in order that Satan might not outwit you. (See 2Cor.2:11). Satan knows the scriptures very well, for this reason; he always uses his intelligence to lure believers to do things which brings God's wrath on His children. Thus, I want to draw the attention of believers to this particular issue which is causing great damage to fellowshipping with God to some believers. Therefore, if someone comes to you for financial or any other assistance, and if you cannot help him, just be faithful to him and let him go his way, may be God will provide another way out for him. Deceiving him to go and come while you know very well you will never give him anything, will cause you much problems in the very near future, because God think about the poor and needy among us. I hope you remember the story of the rich man and the poor man—Lazarus. (Luke 16:19-31).

Years ago, one of the elders in my church handled this issue tactfully and I was very pleased with his action—**A SINCERE LOVE!** One church member and a friend asked me to accompany him to the elder's house to ask for a financial assistance to buy an engine for the taxicab he was driving.

When he became aware the reason for our visit, he replied and openly told my friend, 'I have the money you have requested, but I cannot give it to you. The reason is that this taxi does not belong to you, it is for someone else, you are just a driver and the owner of the car does not know me and I also do not know him.

Secondly, he said in case anything happens and the owner takes back his car away from him, he may lose his money. Lastly, he indicated that anything can happen to the taxicab including mechanical failures which are mostly common in this part of the world'. This was what he told him plainly.

He was given some pocket money and was advised to attend Friday morning prayer session at church. Surprisingly this huge pocket money was offered free of charge to prove the sincerity of his love, to reiterate his reasons for the refusal of the loan and to specify that he meant business in the Lord. The elder requested my opinion on what has done, thinking he has been wronged however. I congratulated and appreciated him for that act of kindness which was a reflection of the SINCERE LOVE the Apostle Peter was drawing believers' attention to. (See 1 Peter 1:22.)

Believers, this is the behavior God expects from us toward our brothers. If someone comes to you for any help and if you can help him just do it and the Lord will be pleased with you. If for some reason you can't, please let him go in peace. It will be wrong to deceive the seeker of help and to have watched him use the little money left on him for transportations to you only to receive nothing.

The elder I just narrated his story to you right now did his best. Anyone who does not fear God or does not know Satan's schemes or tricks may have deceived and turned him away offering nothing to him. If you do that you are not obeying the command of God which Jesus was expecting from believers when He spent some times praying for the unity and love we may show to each other. In doing so, the world may know we are His disciples and that is why we are called, CHRISTIANS! (See John 17:20-26, Acts 11:19-26).

However, the Apostle Paul who knew this advised believers with these Bible passages; "**THE <u>GOAL</u> AT THIS COMMAND IS LOVE WHICH COMES FROM A <u>PURE HEART</u> AND GOOD CONSCIENCE AND A <u>SINCERE LOVE</u>. SOME HAVE WANDERED AWAY FROM THESE AND TURN TO MEANINGLESS TALK". 1Tim.1:5-6**. *"GRACE TO ALL WHO LOVE OUR LORD JESUS CHRIST* ***WITH AN UNDYING LOVE"****. Eph. 6:24.* "I AM NOT COMMANDING YOU, BUT I WANT TO TEST THE **<u>SINCERITY OF YOUR LOVE</u>** BY COMPARING IT WITH THE EARNESTNESS OF OTHERS". 2 Corinthians 8:8.

At this point, I hope readers will understand and practice this commandment in order to receive God's blessing and His fellowship. This gives us an advantage so that Satan might not outwit us, for we are not unaware of his schemes. (2 Cor.2:11).

CHAPTER 8

GOD'S APPOINTED TIME FOR YOU IS THE BEST, YOU NEED PERSEVERANCE TO ACHIEVE

From chapter four of this book and the remaining chapters are all about revealing some deeds, attitudes, behaviors or actions which disrupt believers' fellowship with God. These also give way to the devil to lure believers' into his trap. The devil is always looking for ways and means to trap a believer and bring him down from the grace of God which protects him from being harmed by him (the devil). (See Prov.4:16, 1 John 5:18, Psalm 31:20, Jer.20:11, Heb.13:6, Rom.8:31).

All these passages tell us that if we live in the kindness of God by obeying Him, (Rom.11:22), we are assured of divine protection from the Almighty God and His angels. (See chapter three). In this chapter, we will be considering one thing which is working effectively against believers in their walking with God. This one factor is encapsulated in the heading of this chapter—'GOD'S APPOINTED TIME FOR YOU IS THE BEST, YOU NEED PERSEVERANCE TO ACHIEVE'.

Satan has taken the advantage of the nature of God which most believers are ignorant of to lure them to break down their fellowship with God. One of these characters is; God always works with time. He does not rush to save believers from their unwanted situations, nor does He run late to save them. According to Bible passages, He has promised every believer to be patient and wait for His appointed time to save us from any unwanted circumstances. He has said He will give us our hearts' desire at the right time. *"DELIGHT YOURSELF INTO THE LORD AND HE WILL GIVE YOU THE DESIRE OF YOUR HEART. COMMIT YOUR WAY TO THE LORD, TRUST IN HIM AND HE WILL GIVE YOU THE DESIRE OF YOUR HEART. COMMIT YOUR WAY TO THE LORD, TRUST IN HIM AND HE WILL DO THIS. HE WILL MAKE YOUR RIGHTEOUSNESS SHINE LIKE THE DAWN, THE JUSTICE OF YOUR CAUSE LIKE THE NOONDAY SUN.* ***BE STILL BEFORE THE LORD AND WAIT PATIENLY FOR HIM,*** *DO NOT FRET WHEN MEN SUCCEED IN THEIR WAYS WHEN THEY CARRY OUT THEIR WICKED SCHEMES". Psalm 37:1-11.*

The passage above is full of WILL(s) indicating what has been planned for you or the request yet to be granted at the right time—THE APPOINTED TIME. One musician composed a song and some of the words in the song say; "**God knows what He is doing. If He had created the fish first before creating the sea, where would have been the place for the fish to live?**" But Satan who knows this very nature of God always tries to entice believers to rush and get things done before God's appointed time for them. This move always results in disappointed at the end of their efforts. Due to this, many believers are losing trust and faith in the Lord and this is helping him to steal, destroy and kill these believers who lack knowledge in the Lord.

Believers, who do not know way of the Lord and for that matter cannot wait for His appointed time, always bring problems to themselves and at times to others. While God is preparing and planning something special for His children, the devil also causes them to rush and disrupt God's plan. Let us consider the following passages; *"HOWEVER, AS IT IS WRTTEN: 'WHAT NO EYE HAS SEEN, WHAT NO EAR HAS HEARD, AND WHAT NO HUMAN MIND HAS CONCEIVED—* ***THESE THINGS GOD HAS PREPARED FOR THOSE WHO LOVE HIM".*** *1Corinthians 2:9.*

This is a very powerful passage to confirm this subject. Read on AND GET KNOWLEDGE OF HOW God does thing on your behalf. *"YET THE LORD LONGS TO BE GRACIOUS TO YOU, HE RISES TO SHOW YOU COMPASSION. FOR THE LORD IS A GOD OF JUSTICE.* ***BLESSED ARE ALL WHO WAIT FOR HIM".*** *Isaiah 30:18.* This passage also reminds you to wait and be patient with Him and at the appointed time, He will get the things done for you perfectly. Read on! "*YOU NEED TO PERSEVERE SO THAT WHEN YOU HAVE DONE THE WILL OF GOD, YOU WILL RECEIVE WHAT HE HAS PROMISED". Hebrews 10:36.*

According to Proverbs 4:16, the devils have been trained and sent out by their master Satan, either to entice or lure believers to do what ought not to be done so that their fellowship with God can be disrupted. Therefore, be on your guard!

The duty the Lord has given me to perform in this kingdom's business which every believer has a part to play is to expose the devil's tricks (devices) to believers. (2 Corinthians 2:11). Whoever takes them seriously will be able to overcome them. For this reason, I urge anyone reading this book to be mindful of the contents. Always exercise patience and wait for the Lord's appointed time.

Do you know what God has planned for you? It's here! *"THIS IS WHAT THE LORD SAYS: WHEN SEVENTY YEARS ARE COMPLETED FOR BABYLON, I WILL COME TO YOU AND FULFILL* ***MY GOOD PROMISES*** *TO BRING YOU BACK TO THIS PLACE.* ***FOR I KNOW THE PLANS I HAVE FOR YOU,*** *DECLARES THE LORD,* ***'PLANS TO PROSPER YOU AND NOT TO HARM YOU, PLANS TO GIVE YOU HOPE AND A FUTURE".*** *Jeremiah 29:10-11.* I hope the good lessons in this passage which God is talking about are, His 'GOOD PROMISES' will be fulfilled at the appointed time.

Again, He declares these good promises as 'A plan to prosper you but not to harm you'. Of course, your heavenly Father will not plan anything harmful for you! Whatever we are going through is for our own good, hope and a bright future. I have told you before that when we realize we are dealing with God but not Satan, it gives us the hope that at the end we will come out victorious because our God always have better plans for His children who worship Him faithfully. (See Prov.19:21)

Are you in financial constrains? Still believe in God and wait for Him patiently and at the appointed time, you will come out victorious and the glory will be given to Him. Accept that your God DOES NOT FAIL IN

HIS PROMISE! Therefore never make any attempt to establish any dirty business to make money. Even if you do succeed, it will increase your poverty and your situation will be worst. This can lead you to deny your faith in the Lord and this is the perfect will of your enemy—devil. (See Proverbs.4:16)

Are you also in need of a marriage partner? You need to persevere and when you have done the will of God and remained single for some time, Mr. or Miss right will appear fully prepared without lacking anything in marriage. Some believers ignore this advice and marry anybody who comes their ways and later find themselves in a dangerous relationship. This helps Satan to destroy their holy faith and salvation.

Some believers know it is against God's will to break their marriage, but when they find themselves in a marriage without God's favor, they then gather courage provided by the devil and starts to break it. Some few years ago, an elder who was almost ready to enter into a full time ministry couldn't stand the bad treatment his wife was giving to him. Eventually he broke down the marriage, was suspended in the church and he lost his eldership position.

You need to persevere and when you have done the will of God, you will receive the right woman fully prepared to be a pastor's wife who can support you in the ministry. Jesus said; *"IT'S BETTER TO GO TO HEAVEN WITH ONE HAND THAN TO GO TO HELL WITH BOTH HANDS"*. Matthew 5:29-30. In view of this, bachelors and spinsters in the Lord should rely on the Lord and trust Him to see them through bachelorhood for the sake of your salvation.

Are you in need of children? You also need to persevere and remain in that situation for some time and when you have done the will of God, you will bring forth twins and all the glory will be given to the Most High God. Do not allow anyone used by the devil to confuse and take you to spiritually questionable places with the hope of finding a solution to your child bearing problem.

As a child of God who is unable to have children, it may not be the work of the devil. God may have been responsible for closing your womb for a while for the purposes of revealing his glory. Of course He is the One who closed the wombs of Sarah, Rebecca, Rachel, Hannah, Elizabeth and many mighty women of God for good reasons. Yet after they had done His will, these women who people knew as barren brought forth many mighty men of God, such as Isaac, Jacob, Joseph, Samuel, Gideon and John the Baptist. Check this passage; *"BUT TO HANNAH HE GAVE A DOUBLE PORTION BECAUSE HE LOVED HER,* ***AND THE LORD HAD CLOSED HER WOMB".*** *1 Samuel 1:5.* The underline sentence tells us Hannah's womb was not close by Satan nor any of his accomplices, it was closed by the Almighty God for a good reason to give her hope and bright future. (Jer.29:11, 1 Cor.2:9.)

Apart from these biblical examples we just considered, some believers who devoted themselves fully to serving the Lord in the ministry, could not have any children at all despite their hard work for the Lord in the ministry. The Lord did not open the wombs of their wives until they died unproductively. If these believers did not know the way and the will of God, they could not have accepted it and would have looked for solutions from other sources; **"BUT THE PEOPLE WHO KNOW THEIR GOD SHALL BE STRONG AND DO EXPLOITS". Dan.11:32. (KJV)** However, if you are married for some time now and are without a child of your own, do not call the situation a disgrace. In doing so, you will give the devil an opportunity to deceive and cause you to lose your salvation.

Remind yourself at all times that anyone who cannot wait for God's appointed time brings problems to himself and others. The following are the biblical examples;

(1) ABRAHAM AND SARAH;

"THE LORD SAID TO ABRAM, LEAVE YOUR COUNTRY, YOUR PEOPLE AND YOUR FATHER'S HOUSEHOLD AND GO TO THE LAND I WILL SHOW YOU. I WILL MAKE YOU INTO A GREAT NATION AND I WILL BLESS YOU. I WILL MAKE YOUR NAME GREAT AND YOU WILL BE A BLESSING". Gen.12:1-2. This passage is the call of Abraham and the promise by God to increase and make a great nation out of him. *"WHICH GOD WHO DOES NOT LIE PROMISED BEFORE THE BEGINNING OF TIME,* ***AND AT HIS APPOINTED SEASON HE BROUGHT HIS WORD TO LIGHT".*** *Titus 1:2-3.*

This passage has thrown some light on our subject that at God's own APPOINTED SEASON, the promise He made to the couple was fulfilled.

Abraham believed Him and waited for some time, yet there was no sign that Madam Sarah was going to bear a child to fulfill this great promise. They thought God who neither CANNOT LIE nor whose promise cannot fail had disappointed them. Madam Sarah was able to convince father Abraham to forget about those promises of God, and the result is the birth of the boy Ishmael. (See Gen.16:1-15).

When God's own appointed time came, He fulfilled that old promise He made to them and the result is the birth of the boy Isaac. *"NOW THE LORD WAS GRACIOUS TO SARAH* ***AS HE HAD SAID,*** *AND THE LORD DID FOR SARAH* ***WHAT HE HAD PROMISED.*** *SARAH BECAME PREGNANT AND BORE A SON TO ABRAHAM IN HIS OLD AGE,* ***AT THE VERY TIME GOD HAD PROMISED HIM".*** *Gen.21:1-7.*

My dear reader, all that I'm trying to do in this chapter is to pique your interest to have faith in the Lord no matter what you are going through. Just think of the passage above and consider the bold and underlined words which prove that the God we serve's promises never fail.

When this promise was fulfilled, He supported Sarah's decision compelling Abraham to drive away the illegitimate child and his mother from home. God did this just to prove to Abraham and all believers that He is not a man that He should lie, nor the son of man that He can change His mind from what He had planned to do. The scriptures ask; '**Does He speak and then not act?**' Num.23:19. Again He said; *"I WILL NOT VIOLATE MY COVENANT, OR ALTER WHAT MY LIPS HAVE UTTERED".* Psalm 89:34. What Abraham did brought him an untold distress and a very big problem to the whole world—that is the result of going before God's appointed time. (Gen.21:8-21)

Are you in need of children? You need to persevere, and when you have done the will of God you will definitely receive what He has promised. If it happens to be a little late, still believe and never think negatively of your inability to have children. Don't give Satan the chance to lure you into his trap. (2Cor.2:11). Similarly, the devil can use some people to entice you to lose trust in the Lord. They can help to end up at a questionable place to look for solution. But remember; "*YOU SHALL HAVE NO OTHER GODS BEFORE ME". Exod.20:3-6.*

(2) **JACOB**—Gen.25:19-34, 27:1-46, 28:1-22, 29:1-35, 30:1-end, 32:1-end, 33:1-end.

There is a story in the book I read some time ago which is similar to Jacob's story in the Bible. There was a great warrior in a certain country, his name is Macbeth. His uncle was a king in that country. According to the custom and tradition of the country, the king's oldest son is supposed to succeed him as the next king if he dies or can no longer be the king. Meanwhile, Macbeth was the chief commander of the soldiers who had won all the battles he had fought for the nation. For this reason the king loved him so much and he commanded respect in the whole nation.

However, the king's oldest son was a very little boy who could not rule a nation should his father died at that time. For this reason, Macbeth realized he had a better chance to become the next king if the king died. This ambition sunk deep into his brain and it became his thinking every day. Of course, the devil realized his intensions and wanted to use it to destroy the family and the nation which eventually became successful.

One day, when Macbeth was returning from a great battle he had led his soldiers to win for the nation, the devil met him in the form of three witches. They PROPHESIED in his favor that very soon he would be the next king in the country—this is the same country his uncle was reining as king. According to the customs and traditions of the country, he was not qualified to become a king. Since he was ambitious to become the king, he believed them and when he arrived home, he quickly informed his wife who also was very glad to become a queen. Afterward, they planned how it would be possible for him to become a king to replace his lovely uncle. Meanwhile, the devils who prophesied he would be the next king did not tell him how it would happen. Therefore, his wife (who played the role of Madam Sarah and Jacob's mother-Rebecca) brought the idea to kill the king as soon as possible in order to have the throne at the very time the king's son was a little boy. The plan became successful and the king got murdered secretly by Macbeth and his wife.

When the elders in the country decided to enthrone Macbeth as the next king because the king's son was a minor, the rumor came out that it was Macbeth who murdered the king in order to succeed him as the king. The rumor became a reality and the people of the nation fought against him, they killed him, his supporters and his entire family.

Now, I want you to consider this; WHO WON THE THRONE?—The devil! I hope you will agree with me if Macbeth **KNEW** his unnecessary thinking (ambition) to become a king would eliminated the entire family, he would not have even thought about it. I believe he would have regretted very much at the place of his death his stupid ambition. Believers, this is the very reason I have been urging you not to think negatively of any problem you are going through, because the devil is always at work to entice believers to do what ought not to be done.

Now, what happened to Jacob? Just read the Bible texts I have provided above to see what really happened to him. It is similar to the case of Macbeth and he also faced much more troubles till he died. He rushed through the wrong way to fulfill God's promise in his life and later regretted because he suffered throughout his life on earth.

The story is when Jacob and his brother Esau were in their mother's womb, God revealed to their mother that there were two nations in her womb, but the younger will be greater than the older. The mother kept this in her mind and this made her love the younger son Jacob more than the older son Esau. Their father Isaac also loved the older Esau as the custom demanded, the older is to be blessed but not the younger.

One day when Esau returned from hunting and was very hungry, his brother Jacob had prepared a delicious meal. When Esau asked Jacob to give him some of his food, Jacob shrewdly asked his older brother to first sell his birth-right to him, before he would give him some food to eat. Why did Jacob act that way? Who gave him that idea to ask his brother to sell his birth-right to him in exchange for food?

I want to draw your attention to the fact that achieving God's promise does not need to be done in a dubious or cunning way. Again, Jacob connived with his mother and deceived his father into giving him the blessings which were meant for his older brother Esau. The texts given above illustrates that Jacob encountered numerous troubles as a result of his deception. But see how he replied to Pharaoh, then Egyptian king of his age, when his lovely son Joseph introduced him to the king. *"THEN JOSEPH BROUGHT HIS FATHER JACOB IN AND PRESENTED HIM BEFORE PHARAOH, PHARAOH ASKED HIM,* ***HOW OLD ARE YOU?*** *AND JACOB SAID TO PHARAOH,* ***'THE YEARS OF MY PILGRIMAGE ARE A HUNDRED AND THIRTY. MY YEARS HAVE BEEN FEW AND DIFFICULTY.*** *AND THEY DO NOT EQUAL THE YEARS OF THE PILGRIMAGE OF MY FATHERS".* Gen.47:7-9. According to the passage, all that Jacob wanted to tell pharaoh was that though he was a hundred and thirty years, he had suffered hardships in his life, very few of his years were normal, **the remaining years had been EXTREMELY DIFFICULT**—he could not enjoy the blessings he stole from his brother.

Some preachers and ministers of God do not condemn Jacob's action of intercepting the blessing from his brother, instead, they blame and attack his father Isaac who was about to bless his older son Esau. These preachers believe that Jacob was to be blessed because he was the one promised by God, but Isaac was about to do the wrong thing if Jacob and his mother had not intervened. THIS IS WRONG UNDERSTANDING AND INTERPRETATION OF THE SCRIPTURES! Isaac was only performing his duty as a father and the scriptures did not tell anyone that Esau was a bad boy or a disobedient son and Jacob was a good boy. Definitely Not! Even if we want to trace their record, Jacob was the one who behaved badly. Why did he have to be envious of his brother's eldership and cleverly asked him to sell his birth-right to him in exchanged of food? Was that what God delighted in? The point I want to emphasize here is that we are worshipping a God who DOES NOT LIE! Whatever He says and promises comes to pass. (See Isaiah 46:11, 55:8-11) If it is not so, then, Shadrach, Meshach, and Abed-nego should have changed their minds and worshipped the Golden Image put up to be worshipped by Nebuchadnezzar. Because in their very eyes, the fire was doubled and tripled which could have intimidated them to bow down to that image just to save their lives, but they said, **'We know the God we serve is able to save us from your hand' which He also proved He is always faithful to His promise.** (See Dan.3)

If God cannot do exactly what He says, then, Daniel also should have stopped praying when a decree was made that the lion's den will be a place for anyone who disobeys this decree. But what happened? God proved His might and the glory was given to Him, this makes Him unique from all other gods. (See Dan.6) Someone asked; *"DOES HE SPEAK AND THEN NOT ACT? DOES HE PROMISE AND NOT FULFILL? GOD IS NOT A MAN THAT HE SHOULD LIE, NOR A SON OF MAN, THAT HE SHOULD CHANGE HIS MIND". Num.23:19.* **"THE ONE WHO CALLS YOU IS FAITHFUL AND HE WILL DO IT" 1Thess.5:24.** *"IF WE ARE FAITHLESS, HE WILL* ***REMAIN FAITHFUL*** *FOR HE CANNOT DISOWN HIMSELF". 2Tim.2:13.*

All these passages show God is capable to do anything He says, plans and promises without human's help to achieve any of this. Therefore, whatever situation you find yourself, kindly wait for God's appointed time and He will make your righteousness shine like the noonday sun. (See Psalm 37:1-7).

(3) **SAUL:—1 Samuel 13:1-15.**

We are still trying to find out what happened to some mighty men of God who failed to wait for His appointed time, in order to avoid their fate. The third person for this lesson is King Saul who also rushed to sacrifice burnt offerings for the Lord which he was not supposed to have sacrificed. But he could not wait for Samuel, the priest whose duty, it was to sacrifice burnt offerings to the Lord but not the king. Because of this, God rejected him as king and sent Samuel to anoint David as the next king to replace him. *"YOU ACTED FOOLISHLY, SAMUEL SAID. YOU HAVE NOT KEPT THE COMMAND THE LORD YOUR GOD GAVE YOU; IF YOU HAD, HE WOULD HAVE ESTABLISHED OVER ISRAEL FOR ALL TIME. BUT NOW YOUR KINGDOM WILL NOT ENDURE; THE LORD HAS SOUGHT OUT A MAN AFTER HIS OWN HEART AND APPOINTED HIM LEADER OF HIS PEOPLE, BECAUSE YOU HAVE NOT KEPT THE LORD'S COMMAND". 1Sam.13:13-14.*

Once again, I want to remind believers that no matter what situation you find yourself in, never put the plans and the promises of God aside and act to save yourself from that situation. Rather, wait patiently for His appointed time and He will surely not let you down. Even if it will cause you to die, it's better to die and save your soul, than to disobey His word which can cause you problems and will give the devil access to steal you and destroy you. (See Rev.2:10-11, John 10:10) I am giving you these tips of how Satan is able to subdue a believer and take him away from the presence of God. All they (Devils) do is to entice or lure believers to do what they ought not to do!

All the three people I have cited in our lesson were in critical conditions which caused them to act before God's appointed time. In the case of Abraham, he was 75 years old when God called and promised him He would make him a great nation. (Gen.12:1-9) He believed God alright at that time, but waiting for eleven years afterwards without a child pushed him to accept his wife's decision to impregnate her Egyptian maidservant, Hagar. With this act he fathered the boy Ishmael when he was 86 years old. (See Gen.16:1-16) Abraham did his best and waited for God up to 86 years, but when he was facing pressure from his wife, he yielded to sleeping with Hagar and the result is the boy through whom the whole world is under fire. (See Gal.4:21-27.)

Also in the case of Jacob, although his father was ready to bless Esau, he believed himself to be more deserving of the blessings because he was obviously aware of the promise God made to their mother. So she purposed in her mind that when it came to the time of blessing that Jacob would be blessed instead of Esau. (See Gen.25:23). That is why Jacob and his mother plotted to deceive Isaac to receive the blessings in a deceitful way that caused him many troubles. In fact, even Jacob who received the blessing could not enjoy it, instead, he encountered problem upon problems. Jacob would have had a better outcome if had been bold enough to tell his father that he had come for the promised blessings since Esau had previously sold his birth right to him. And the mother should have added that the Lord promised to bless the younger but not the older. If they had been able to tell the truth, the Lord would have intervened and the right thing would have been done. *"I SAW HEAVEN STANDING OPEN AND THERE BEFORE ME WAS A WHITE HORSE, WHOSE RIDER* ***IS CALLED FAITHFUL AND TRUE. WITH JUSTICE, HE JUDGES AND MAKES WAR".*** *Rev.19:11.*

Believers should learn to wait patiently for God's appointed time and He will surely not let them down. At times you may be right in your own eyes and even get support from your loved ones, but do not allow the situation you find yourself in to cause you to abandon the plans and promises of God in search of your own solutions. May be, you are the only daughter of your parents and they want you to get married and give them grandchildren, but at 35 years and over, you are still without a husband. I can see the pressure you may encounter from your impatient parents. Sometimes they may force you to marry someone who might not be God's choice for you and cannot love you to the very end of your life. But in all, you need to persevere and when you have done the will of God, you will receive the promise—GOOD THINGS THAT LAST FOREVER! (1Cor.2:9, John 16:20-23, Heb.10:35-39). Remind yourself that the devil is always at work to get you away from the love of God which protects you from them.

Again you may have been married for many years and have not even got a single child and you are under tremendous pressure from your parents and in-laws, who are constantly demanding that you give them their grand-children. At times, your immature husband may join them in maltreating you or even divorce you in order to marry someone else, but in all these, be still and silent before the Lord and see how He will be gracious to you and glorify you. Never allow any of them to take you to any questionable places to look for a solution from other sources. Hold on to your holy faith, and when you have done the will of God, you will receive what He has promised—GOOD THINGS THAT LAST FOREVER! (Heb.10:36, James 1:16-17)

Again, someone also may be in critical financial constrains, you also need to be persevere. Do not try to put the word of God aside and try to make money from anywhere, accept the word of God in good faith and remember what has been promised in a situation like this; "KEEP YOUR LIFE FREE FROM THE LOVE OF MONEY AND BE CONTENT WITH WHAT YOU HAVE, BECAUSE GOD HAS SAID, NEVER WILL I LEAVE YOU, NEVER WILL I FORSAKE YOU. SO WE SAY WITH CONFIDENCE THE LORD IS MY HELPER, I WILL NOT BE AFRAID, WHAT CAN A MAN DO TO ME?" Heb.13:5-6. (Also read this text for more enlightenment; 1Sam.2:7-9)

Concluding this chapter, I still want to remind readers of how our enemy Satan is using these acts to outwit many believers. For this reason, try as much as possible not to be his victim, no matter the situation you find yourself in, you need to persevere and bear in mind that you have a very big God who is always by your side and never fails His children who put their trust in Him. (See Rom.10:11, Isaiah 49:14-17) Therefore, do not throw away your confidence in Him because it will be richly rewarded. (Also read the following texts to refresh your memory; Heb.10:35-39, Je r.1:12, 29:10-14, Isaiah 55:7-12, Prov.19:21, 1Sam.2:7-9, Psalm 102:12-13, 119:126, John 16:20-23, 17:1, Gal.4:4-6). All these texts will tell you that God never fails to fulfill His promises but He works in His own TIME!

CHAPTER 9

CHOOSING A MARRIAGE PARTNER

We are still trying to figure out some of the things the devil uses to lure or entice believers to rebel against God, which gives him a great advantage over those erring believers. One thing he is greatly using to bring believers down is breaking up their marriages—DIVORCE! We also learned in chapter one of this book, since he became God's enemy, he always opposes whatever God does and attacks it. It was God who instituted marriage and blessed it for man and woman to enjoy it. (See Gen.2:18-25) But now, can we truly say that married couples are really enjoying themselves in their marriages? After marriage was instituted, God said; ***"I HATE DIVORCE, AND I HATE IT WHEN PEOPLE CLOTHE THEMSELVES WITH INJUSTICE, SAYS THE LORD ALMIGHTY. SO BE ON YOUR GUARD, AND DO NOT BE UNFAITHFUL".*** Mal.2:16. (See Mal.2:14-16)

I hope you will do well to stop or avoid doing things your loved one does not like. Since God is our heavenly Father who takes care of us and protects us from the devils' treats and attempts to harm us, should we not avoid divorce because He hates it—DISLIKES? Therefore, we are considering the lose-holes which are causing problems in our marriages which are supposed to be a blessing to Christian couples. The first thing that causes this problem to starts stems from how we choose our spouses, thus, this chapter deals with how to choose a marriage partner as a believer.

It has been arranged by God for every believer to marry to fulfill His purpose for His children here on this earth. He said; *"IT IS NOT GOOD FOR A MAN TO BE ALONE. I WILL MAKE A* ***HELPER SUITABLE FOR HIM".*** *Gen.2:18*. God Himself has accepted that being a single person without a wife cannot help any genuine Christian man. Therefore every Christian has got a responsibility to marry to fulfill God's plan for instituting marriage. Of course, He did not institute marriage just for nothing, but a good purpose indeed! But before one can marry, he must choose a partner SUITABLE for him.

Unfortunately, choosing a suitable partner is where the devil and his accomplices are dominating, confusing, leading and deceiving believers to choose the wrong partners, instead of those who may be suitable for them. This chapter therefore deals with how to choose a partner suitable for you. How can one know that this or that woman will be suitable for him? According to the word of God, those who are guided by God, the institutor of marriage can easily find a suitable helper as wife. (See Gen.2:18-24) However, in order for you to be guided to the right woman and man who can best suit you, then you need a consultation.

THE CONSULTATION

In some parts of some countries, we have heard that before a man will make a choice of a marriage partner, his parents need to consult someone who knows very much about the family which their son wants to marry from. If they find something wrong with that family, they quickly withdraw their intention and advise their son of the danger of the step he wanted to take in life. This is carnal or physical consultation which is no longer recognized in some parts of the world among the people who believe in the Lord Jesus Christ as their Lord and personal savior. Physically, there may not be any problem but spiritually, there may be a demon possessed person in the family to torment their marriage in the very near future.

On the other hand, the consultations to find the right person to marry cannot be taken away or ignored completely from our marriage system. Without consultation, it will be very difficult to get a suitable partner. Therefore, as Christians, the one you must consult is the God Almighty, who is Omniscient, Omnipresent and Omnipotent. He knows everyone's heart and every family's background, both physically and spiritually. It is very important that believers take this advice and consult God when they are choosing partners, because there is a condition attached to marriage which forbids divorce no matter how you are being treated. This means if you enter into it, it becomes imperative to stay in it till death separates you from your spouse.

Satan knows all these conditions attached to marriage and the consequence if anyone dishonors these conditions in marriage. Therefore I want to help the unmarried believers to do everything possible to avoid being married to the wrong persons. If you make a wrong choice, you can never correct it, unless you ignore the word of God. However, when you ignore the word of God, it becomes rebellion against Him which can lead you to be disciplined as we have studied already. (Isaiah 63:10, Heb.12:4-11, 10:26, 27, 31, 6:4-6)

Sometime ago, a certain pastor's wife fell sick and was at the point of death. She had been admitted at the hospital for a while but her condition did not improve and it seemed like she may never survive from that sickness. A miracle happened and she got well and was about to be discharged. An elder of the church happily went to inform the reverend minister that his wife was to be discharged shortly. The pastor was shocked of this news and inadvertently exclaimed; '**SO MY WIFE DID NOT DIE!**' When the elder asked him why he was not happy about his wife's recovery, he replied that he had made a mistake by choosing her for a wife and she has been tormenting his life. He thought he would have an opportunity to make a better choice this time with her demise. Unfortunately, SHE DID NOT DIE!—SHE SURVIVED! He believed she was coming back to continue her disturbances and torture him again. This news soon reached the senior ministers who quickly suspended him from the ministry. This is one of the results of having made a wrong choice in marriage.

A certain elder also made a wrong choice and he is now reaping the results. He lost his job a few months after he had a great wedding. His wife who seemed to have been sent by the devil took advantage of it and punished him severely. For more than two years, his wife had not prepared any food for him. She just cooked for herself without bothering to share it with her husband. It was a certain sister in the church who was assisting him with some meals and money sometimes. If this wife was not giving her husband any food to eat, then you can imagine what was happening between the two of them in the bed room for those two years. Oh, sorry Elder! Making a mistake in choosing a marriage's partner can lead to untold problems such as those stated above. Even some believers have lost their salvation through mistakes they made when they were choosing their marriage partners.

While the pastor was expecting his wife to die, the elder was also planning to break up God's condition attached to marriage—DIVORCE! (See Mal.2:16) He was planning to divorce that ungrateful wife. But is it possible for an elder of the church to divorce his wife? I know this question can be easily answered "YES" by some believers because of how they understand and interpret the Bible. We have believers who are worshipping God alright but do not fear Him. If you are one of such people, your answer will be "YES". Again, we have some believers who fear God and respect Him so much, but they lack knowledge in the word of God, for this reason they have been carried away by erroneous teachings. (Hosea 4:6, Ephe.4:14) Therefore, based on what their ministers have taught them, they can also answer "YES" to that question. But those who are being led by the Spirit of God and obey the word of God will answer differently. Although this elder's case is a very sad story, but for the sake of maintaining his fellowship with God and salvation, these believers will not encourage him to divorce that wicked and ungrateful wife. (Mal.2:16) Believers, as far as your salvation is concerned, you need to consult our God Almighty, the Omnipresent and Omniscient in order to be guided to choose a suitable partner.

What is happening to the men who have made a wrong choice is also happening to some women who have also allowed themselves to be carried away by the wrong partners. A certain School/Sunday school female teacher was married to a young man in the church, who seemed to have been sent by the devil purposely to destroy her Christian faith. Soon after their marriage, that man began behaving like an unbeliever, beating this beautiful wedded and educated woman. After this treatment, he traveled without informing her of his destination. In fact, nobody could trace his whereabouts and some speculated that he might have travelled abroad. The woman did not know what to do, either she should go ahead and divorce him in his absence, or she should wait for him. But the question was, she was to wait until when? Perhaps, he may not return to the country again because he is a foreigner. Even if he comes back, what is he going to do to her? Maltreatment!

Coincidentally, I chanced upon this man one day in Accra, Ghana West Africa and asked him, where have you been my friend all this while? He started laughing and told me he was in hurry so he would call and talk to me later. I asked him, where he was going that he could not spend a few minutes of his time with me? He answered that he was about to be married and his people were waiting for him. I inquired again, but what about the wife you left behind, have you had a divorced? He responded, she died a while back. Oh! This woman had thought of her husband's sudden disappearance and died as a result of that and here is this man happily preparing to marry again. Spinsters in the Lord, making a wrong choice without consulting the Omniscient and Omnipresent God can bring problem such as these. As a lady in Christ, you need to consult God properly before accepting any proposal. But our women sometimes hastily accept proposals if they realize that the man is financially sound or very handsome. But money and beauty cannot promote a good marriage.

You may also know some believers who are facing similar problems for the mistakes they made with their choices. In fact, there are lots of problems for those who choose wrong partners without consulting God, and it is the work of the devil to entice or lure believers to rebel against God. Therefore, if you have not as yet entered into marriage, then, try to practice these tips I am giving you in this book in order that Satan might not outwit you. (See 2Cor.2:11)

In fact, some believers may not understand me properly, because breaking up a marriage is not a difficult task for them. To them, it is like counting 1, 2, and 3, because of where they come from, their customs, traditions and how they were trained up. But in Christianity, we are using the same Bible and are serving the same God who said, "**I HATE DIVORCE**!" (Mal.2:16, Eph.4:2-6) Believer having a divorce in the sight of God is like committing adultery, murder, stealing, slandering and the likes. (See 1Cor.6:9-11, Gal.5:19-21, James 2:11.) "**OR DO YOU NOT KNOW**

THAT WRONGDOERS WILL NOT INHERIT THE KINGDOM OF GOD? DO NOT BE DECIVED!" 1Cor.6:9. *"WHOEVER HAS EARS, LET THEM HEAR WHAT THE SPIRIT SAYS TO THE CHURCHES. TO THOSE WHO ARE VICTORIOUS, I WILL GIVE THE RIGHT TO EAT FROM THE TREE OF LIFE, WHICH IS IN THE PARADISE OF GOD". Rev.2:7.*

CHAPTER 10

THE IMPORTANCE OF PRAYERS

We have realized through our lesson in the previous chapter that, before a believer can make a rightful choice in marriage, he/she must consult the Omniscient God who sees and knows everything and everyone's behavior. This chapter deals with how one can consult God. It is through prayers!

It is God who created you and knows who is suitable for you. Therefore, take enough time to pray about your marriage, right from the very first day you plan to marry. Of course, you must be serious about it because the devil is enticing many believers to rebel against God's will through unexpected divorce which is the abomination of God. (See Mal.2:14-16) Submit your desires and expectations to God in prayers, and He will give you the desire of your heart. (See Psalm 37:4-6, James 1:16-17)

According to the scriptures, when God created the woman out of a man, He did not leave them and go, but HE BROUGHT HER TO THE MAN, and the man was very pleased and satisfied with what God gave him. (See Gen.2:18-23). This tells us that God is committed to ensuring that His trusted believers get the suitable partners so that they can enjoy a good marriage. Therefore, believers should learn to allow God to guide them in choosing suitable partners through prayers, instead of making the choice first before bringing these partners to Him for His approval.

The Christians who follow their hearts and choose spouses by themselves, have slim chances of getting suitable spouses just like the unbelievers, because Satan always influences their motions and personal desire. At times, some of the unbelievers also get good and suitable spouses and enjoy good marriages till death separates them, but they do not have God's blessing in their marriages. I call this type of marriage; **'A BY CHANCE OR RAFFLE MARRIAGE'**. If misfortune hits and there is no perfect understanding between them, then they feel free to divorce and try someone else. This may continue until they find the one suitable for them. That is why you may see some children who have the same mother but have different fathers. Some of them may also have the same father but different mothers, because their father was trying his luck to get the one suitable for him.

I want to remind believers that God has given us our will—this means He does not force believers to do anything against their will. If a believer depends on God, He will see him through, but if he opts to do things on his own, God will let him do it without interfering. What most people call love—"I love him or I love her," may not really be the love which sustains and promotes good marriage. It is or may be LUST! This lust is also known as 'ROMANTIC OR INFATUATION LOVE'. Though, you may have a strong feeling which seems to be a great love for a woman or man because of their appearances, if you go ahead and marry that individual, this marriage may not survive. Believers who choose their spouses through romantic or infatuation soon find their marriages ending up on the rock, because it has no good foundation.

Others advice not to marry from this or that tribe, rich or poor, short or tall, fat or slim. In Africa, some people even warn the unmarried not to marry anyone who comes from a rich or poor family, or anyone who is highly educated than they are and so many other reasons best known to them. I want believers to know in this lesson that all these advices are the deceitful ways of the devil to alternate God's choice for you and to put you into problematic marriages.

Again, those who are praying about their marriages should not think much about their personal desires else they may not see when God grants their requests. As you may be thinking and expecting to get married to a fair in complexion individual, the Lord may have this dark in complexion fearful and respectful individual who will be ideal for you. Thus, it is advisable to continue praying until your prayer is answered.

Unfortunately, some believers do not know why their prayers are not being answered by God. When they do not receive exactly what they ask for in their prayers, they just go ahead and marry anyone of their choice. These carnal Christians later find themselves in much trouble giving the devil the opportunity to outwit them from the grace of God. Therefore be mindful of the following points on how to pray in the right direction to be heard and answered by God.

HOW TO PRAY

The following points will help and remind you of what prevents your prayers from being answered as well as what you must do to make your prayer more acceptable to God. I am reminding you because although I know you may have prior knowledge about these points, you may not take them seriously, therefore watch them!

HUMILITY—*"IF MY PEOPLE WHO ARE CALLED BY MY NAME WILL HUMBLE THEMSELVES AND PRAY AND SEEK MY FACE AND TURN FROM THEIR WICKED WAYS, THEN I WILL HEAR FROM HEAVEN AND WILL FORGIVE THEIR SIN AND HEAL THEIR LAND".* 2Chron.7:14.

A Christian who is praying to God must humble himself before Him. He must pray with a broken-heart, and pray for the forgiveness of sins committed and turn away from them. Humility before God in prayer means to pray with FASTING AND WITH A BROKEN-HEART. **"I PROCLAIMED A FAST, SO THAT WE MIGHT HUMBLE OURSELVES BEFORE OUR GOD!" Ezra 8:21**.

FORGIVENESS—Before your prayer can be accepted and answered, you must forgive those who have wronged you. *"AND WHEN YOU STAND PRAYING IF YOU HOLD ANYTHING AGAINST ANYONE, FORGIVE HIM SO THAT YOUR FATHER IN HEAVEN MAY FORGIVE YOU YOUR SIN".* Mark 11:25.

A certain sister in the church had been praying and fasting for a long time concerning a very important issue, but she had not received the answer to her prayers. One day she came to ask me about why Christians at times have difficulties receiving answers to their prayer requests from God? She added that "I have been praying tirelessly with fasting without living in sin, yet, God does not answer my prayers." I told her to turn her Bible to Romans 3:1-4, verse 4 reads; **"NOT AT ALL! LET GOD BE TRUE AND EVERY HUMAN BE A LIAR"**. After sharing this Bible passage with her, I then asked her to be frank with herself and with God; did she have anything against anybody? She soon recollected and confessed that she had an unresolved conflict with one of her neighbors and she seemed justified. I told her that with God it does not matter who is right or wrong, all He wants His worshippers to know and do is; "IF POSSIBLE, WE SHOULD MAKE EVERYTHING POSSIBLE TO LIVE IN PEACE WITH ALL MEN". Heb.12:14. This is the will of God and as a child of God, if you disobey His commands accordingly regarding forgiveness for those who offend you, all your prayers including 'DRY FASTING' (that is going without food and water for days or weeks in prayers), **will not move God to answer a prayer which comes from a heart filled with grievances**. She was advised to go and peacefully settle the grudge she was bearing that person. When she took my advice and did exactly what I told her, peace was made with that person. She came to me again a few days later with a smile on her face informing me that she had received the answer to the request she had long been praying about.

Believers, these pieces of teachings I am offering in this book will work for you unbelievably if you practice them seriously. Additionally, if you are also praying about your marriage or anything else, kindly forgive your offenders and pray fervently with a pure heart and see how gracious He will be to you as soon as He hears your cry. (See Isaiah 30:19).

RUMINATING: Any believer who prays to God about a specific request, but finds his mind meditating on unnecessary things may not receive the answer to his prayers. "**IF I HAD CHERISHED SIN IN MY HEART, THE LORD WOULD NOT HAVE LISTENED TO ME". Psalm 66:18.**

If your mind and heart are not focusing on God and your requests in moments of prayer, your request may not be granted no matter how long you pray. Hence, do not cherish iniquity in your heart while praying. Our Lord God wants to reason with serious believers and not those who need Him just for a while. Check this passage; "*SHOUT IT ALOUD, DO NOT HOLD BACK. RAISE YOUR VOICE LIKE A TRUMPET. DECLARE TO MY PEOPLE* ***THEIR REBELLION*** *AND TO THE HOUSE OF JACOB* ***THEIR SINS****. FOR DAY AFTER DAY THEY SEEK ME OUT; THEY SEEM EAGER TO KNOW MY WAYS, AS IF THEY WERE A NATION THAT DOES WHAT IS RIGHT AND HAVE NOT FORSAKEN THE COMMAND OF ITS GOD.* ***THEY ASK ME FOR JUST DECISIONS AND SEEM EAGER FOR GOD TO COME NEAR THEM****. WHY HAVE WE FASTED; THEY SAY, AND YOU HAVE NOT SEEN IT? WHY HAVE WE* ***HUMBLED*** *OURSELVES, AND YOU HAVE NOT NOTICED?* ***YET ON THE DAY OF YOUR FASTING, YOU DO AS YOU PLEASE AND EXPLOIT ALL YOUR WORKERS. YOUR FASTING ENDS IN QUARRELING AND STRIFE****, AND IN STRIKING EACH OTHER WITH WICKED FISTS. YOU CANNOT FAST AS YOU DO TODAY AND EXPECT YOUR VOICE TO BE HEARD ON HIGH.* ***IS THIS THE KIND OF FAST I HAVE CHOSEN, ONLY A DAY FOR PEOPLE TO HUMBLE THEMSELVES****? IS IT ONLY FOR BOWING ONE'S HEAD LIKE A REED AND FOR LYING IN SACKCLOTH AND ASHES?* ***IS THAT WHAT YOU CALLED A FAST, A DAY ACCEPTABLE TO THE LORD?"*** Isaiah 58:1-5. (Isaiah 58:1-12) I can see this passage has spoken powerfully to you about some of the things we do to prevent our prayers from being answered by our loving God. The passage has emphasized on fasting as a means of humility before God in prayers, but it should be done in a rightful attitude.

NEGATIVE THOUGHTS: *"DO NOT BE ANXIOUS ABOUT ANYTHING, BUT IN EVERYTHING BY PRAYER AND PETITION WITH THANKSGIVING PRESENT YOUR REQUEST TO GOD. AND THE PEACE OF GOD WHICH TRANSCENDS ALL UNDERSTANDING WILL GUARD YOUR MINDS AND YOUR HEARTS IN CHRIST JESUS"*. Phil.4:4-7.

In this passage we learn that regardless of how situations turn out, it is absolutely irrelevant to entertain negative thoughts such as; 'this sickness will kill me, or now that I am old who will marry me?, or how can I give birth at this age?, and other negative thoughts. If you find yourself in a desperate situation, try to feed yourself with some Bible passages which speaks positively; ***"IS ANYTHING TOO HARD FOR THE LORD? I WILL RETURN TO YOU AT THE APPOINTED TIME NEXT YEAR AND SARAH WILL HAVE A SON"*** Gen.18:14.

As a believer, you must always see victory ahead of you, because though we may be tried, but never shall we be put to shame! (See Rom.10:11, Phil.1:29-30, 1Peter 1:6-7) No matter what you are going through, still believe that come what may, you are VICTORIOUS!

<u>FAITH:</u> *"THEREFORE, I TELL YOU, WHATEVER YOU ASK FOR IN PRAYERS, BELIEVE THAT YOU HAVE RECEIVED IT, AND IT WILL BE YOURS"*. Mark 11:24. *"BUT WHEN HE ASKS, HE MUST BELIEVE AND NOT DOUBT, BECAUSE HE WHO DOUBT IS LIKE A WAVE OF THE SEA BLOWN AND TOSSED BY WIND. THAT MAN SHOULD NOT THINK HE WILL RECEIVE ANYTHING FROM GOD; HE IS A DOUBLE-MINDED MAN, UNSTABLE IN ALL HE DOES"*. James 1:6-8.

These two passages indicate that if you do not believe that your request has been granted, then do not pray at all! This is true because God cannot grant any prayer request without faith

<u>CONFIDENCE:</u> *"LET US THEN APPROACH THE THRONE OF GRACE* ***WITH CONFIDENCE****, SO THAT WE MAY RECEIVE MERCY AND FIND GRACE TO HELP US IN OUR TIME OF NEED"*. Heb.4:16.

There are still some believers whose prayers are **'I am Adam's descendant, and for that matter, I was conceived and born in sin'**. If you still recognize yourself as Adam's descendant, definitely you can never pray with confidence. Without praying in confidence, no matter how long you pray, you will receive nothing. If you still see yourself as Adam's descendant, then it means you are not saved and are still a SINNER! If you are one of these people, kindly take your Bible and read the Book of Romans and the gospel of John in order to identify yourself and your status properly. Those of us who are in Christ Jesus, there is NO CONDEMNATION and we are not Adam's descendant, but children of the Almighty God and co-heirs with Christ Jesus. You will find all these secrets of our happiness and confidence in Christ from the texts I have given you.

EFFECTIVE PRAYER: *"THEREFORE CONFESS YOUR SINS TO EACH OTHER AND PRAY FOR EACH OTHER SO THAT YOU MAY BE HEALED.* ***THE PRAYER OF A RIGHTEOUS MAN IS POWERFUL AND EFFECTIVE****. ELIJAH WAS A MAN LIKE US. HE PRAYED EARNESTLY THAT IT WOULD NOT RAIN FOR THREE AND HALF YEARS. AGAIN, HE PRAYED AND HEAVEN GAVE RAIN, AND THE EARTH PRODUCED IT CROPS".* James 5:16-18.

What is an EFFECTIVE PRAYER? According to the passage, there are two definitions of 'effective' prayer. (i) A prayer of a righteous man who has faithfully confessed his sins committed unintentionally to God, and (ii) A believer who has faithfully confessed his sins committed unintentionally to a 'TRUSTED' prayer partner, who has interceded powerfully and effectively for him.

A church brother narrated his experience this way. He said he had a girlfriend in school that was from a rich family. This girl used to assist him financially. When they graduated from school, that girl vanished from this world. He also converted into Christianity, loved God dearly and desisted from all those immoral lifestyle. At some point in life, he faced some serious financial difficulties. He and his prayer partner fasted and prayed for two weeks, and by God's grace their praying experience ended successfully. When he was about to cook some food to break his fasting, somebody knocked at his door. He opened the door and it was his missing long-time lover who looked very beautiful and attractive. Where have you been all these years? He asked. To abroad, she replied. After a short conversation, he briefed her of his new life experience in Christ as a true believer. This automatically meant that the kind of lifestyles they used to lead cannot be continued anymore.

Upon hearing the news of being born again, she picked up her bag, said good bye, and requested permission to leave. He asked, so you won't give me any money? She said, how can I give you money since we are no longer lovers? I'm going to look for someone else who can make me feel like a woman but not you Mr. born again, she stepped out and left.

According to him, when he saw this woman, he thought she was an answer to his two weeks prayer and fasting, that she had come at the right time to help him of his financial difficulty. He convinced himself to go after her and see if perhaps God may have touched her heart to help him with some money. He chased, found, and brought her back to his room. To cut a long story short, when he tried to convince her to help him with some money, they ended up exchanging words, and before he could realize, she had embraced him, kissed him seriously and held his manhood.

In a twinkle of an eye, he had finished having sex with her. Now this is what happened afterwards. The aftermath of this encounter is precisely the scheme of the enemy I have been cautioning believers about all this while in this book. Immediately they had finished the love-making, she presented a huge sum of money which could even buy a car to him. She did that because she had got what she was sent for.

According to him, he could not handle the money, so he directed her to put it on the bed. It was as if he had been bound in chains. He could not sit down but rather stood still until the lady had said good bye to him and left. His prayer partner immediately felt uncomfortable and noticed something may have gone wrong with his friend. He rushed to his house and found him standing straight with his hands folded at his back.

After faithfully confessing exactly what had happened, his friend prayed powerfully to release him from that bondage he had ended up in. Immediately after his friend had prayed for him, he felt released and when he became aware of himself he wept bitterly and thanked God for saving him from the trap of the devil.

This is a good example of the passage we read earlier encouraging us to pray effectively. (James 5:16-18) Every prayer must be effective before it can be answered. If this man had not confessed his sin to his friend, the devil would have taken him captive. Consequently he would have continued sinning and would have faced God's discipline which could have released him to the devil. Therefore believers must faithfully confess their sins to their prayer partners and pray effectively for each other. Please be advised never to betray him if he confides in you and confesses his sins to you. Instead, understand that no one is perfect. I have said it before that no one can live in this satanic controlled world and never sin. Whoever you are and whatever position you hold in church, at times you may go amiss. (See Eccl. 7:16-20, Rom.3:3-4, 1 John 1:8-10, Heb.4:15)

PRAY ACCORDING TO GOD'S WILL:—*"THIS IS THE CONFIDENCE WE HAVE IN APPROACHING GOD THAT IF WE ASK ANYTHING ACCORDING TO HIS WILL, HE HEARS US".* 1 John 5:14. Some believers spend so much time to pray even with fasting, but they do not receive anything from God, because they do not pray according to the word of God. Therefore, your prayer must be compared to the word of God. *"THEREFORE DO NOT BE FOOLISH BUT UNDERSTAND WHAT THE LORD'S WILL IS"* Eph.5:17.

DO NOT PRAY WITH WRONG MOTIVE:—*"WHEN YOU ASK, YOU DO NOT RECEIVE, BECAUSE YOU ASK WITH WRONG MOTIVES, THAT YOU MAY SPEND WHAT YOU GET ON YOUR PLEASURE"*. James 4:3. This passage shows you the reason your prayers are not answered, because you pray with the wrong motive but not with the will of God. This is why you need to let the word of God dwell in you richly in order to help you to pray without wrong motives but according to the will of God.

PRAY IN JESUS' NAME:—Finally, your prayer must be stamped with the name of Jesus. *"AND I WILL DO WHATEVER YOU ASK IN MY NAME, SO THAT THE SON MAY BRING GLORY TO THE FATHER. YOU MAY ASK ME FOR EVERYTHING IN MY NAME AND I WILL DO IT".* John 14:13-14. **"I TELL YOU THE TRUTH; MY FATHER WILL GIVE YOU WHATEVER YOU ASK IN MY NAME. UNTIL NOW YOU HAVE NOT ASKED ANYTHING IN MY NAME, ASK AND YOU WILL RECEIVE AND YOUR JOY WILL BE COMPLETED"**. John 16:23-24.

Jesus is complaining in the passage that you are praying a lot, but all these prayers are outside his name. Truly, any prayer that is not in His name does not come to Him or His Father and for that matter cannot be answered. It's beyond His territory. When He or the Father receives a prayer that is in His name, He answers on condition that you are able to practice all these guidelines I have given to you. Put them into practice and pray about your marriage plans and any other concern. Present your request to Him and the peace of God which transcends all understanding will guard your heart and your mind in Christ Jesus. (See Phil.4:4-7).

CHAPTER 11

HOW GOD GIVES A SUITABLE MARRIAGE PARTNER

When a believer surrenders his life to God and submits his personal desire and marriage plan to Him in prayers as we have discussed, God now has a duty to perform and that is to give him the desire of his heart—A SUITABLE SPOUSE! Unfortunately, some believers are losing their suitable partners chosen for them by God through the lack of knowledge. (Hosea 4:6) This is because the direction they expect their answers to come from may unexpectedly differ from God's direction. (Jer.29:11) ***"MANY ARE THE PLANS IN A HUMAN HEART, BUT IT IS THE LORD'S PURPOSE THAT PREVAILS".*** **Prov.19:21.** For this reason, let's consider these points of how God gives a SUITABLE PARTNERS.

RECOMMENDATION

Recommendation in marriage is when someone introduces—recommends a person to another person which can be guaranteed as a good spouse. In the same way, God also grants some believers the wisdom to recommend certain people to some believers who intend to marry and who may have prayed about it. Mostly the successful marriages I know were arranged through such recommendations.

Similarly, God can direct someone to recommend someone to you if you have prayed for His guidance. Honestly, you are not bound by the recommendation, but in order that you may not ignore God's choice for you, pray and consider it carefully before you make a final decision. In order to identify whether or not the devil has a hand in it, do not rush to accept or reject it because of the appearance of the person, but pray about it for some time before you give you respond.

Satan and his evil spirits are always everywhere to confuse and deceive believers to marry the wrong partners. So set a special time aside for prayers if someone is recommended to you and consider the issue carefully as you continue praying. The most important thing to do at this juncture is to put your personal desire and expectation away, because God works in mysterious ways. The devil is also very cunning in influencing our desire and emotion. It will be very helpful if you do not delay the response to the right recommendation or the true proposal. But if you have no inner conviction about such a recommendation and if you are absolutely convinced it is not your personal desires and expectations then, do not rush to marry just because she is beautiful or very rich or handsome. Instead, you must continue praying until you become convinced before you response positively to that recommendation. If that person is the suitable partner for you, you will have the peace of mind concerning him or her.

Some believers used to make excuses that; 'I have prayed but have not seen anything'. If you have invested time into prayer concerning your future spouse and still have not seen or heard any response to your prayer, then check yourself if you are in a fellowship with God. *"FOR THE EYES OF THE LORD ARE ON RIGHTEOUS AND **HIS EARS ARE ATTENTIVE TO THEIR PRAYERS**, BUT THE FACE OF THE LORD IS AGAINST THOSE WHO DO EVIL".* 1 Peter 3:12.

CIRCUMSTANCES

God sometimes gives direction through circumstances, but in many cases, He uses this circumstance in the life of believers who sometimes refuse to accept His direction and guidance. "*THIS IS WHAT THE LORD SAYS; STAND AT THE CROSSROADS AND LOOK; ASK FOR THE ANCIENT PATH, ASK WHERE THE GOOD WAY IS, AND WALK IN IT, AND YOU WILL FIND REST FOR YOUR SOULS. BUT YOU SAID, WE WILL NOT WALK IN IT".* Jer.6:16.

This passage shows there are some believers who have their own choice. The Lord knows that these choices may not help them but they also want to satisfy themselves with their personal desire. When it happens this way, it then becomes a struggle with God, and if the believer is being led by the Spirit of God, this will continue until he surrenders and submits to God's guidance.

I know some believers will try to argue about this point because they have been taught that God has given us the free will, so what is the essence of surrendering to His will or direction? Of course, you are right, but also remember that scripture says; "***Those who are being led by the Spirit of God are the children of God"***. Rom.8:14. Our heavenly Father is not an irresponsible Father like Eli who watched his children turn into bad boys. I have already explained that anyone being born of God must hold Him accountable for anything happens in his or her life and count Satan out.

If God were to allow anyone to go the way he wants and later encounters a problem, how will he get to know God?—INJUSTICE!

Of course He has given us our own will, but does it mean He should watch you go astray? No way! When Paul and his companions wanted to travel and preach at Phrygia and Galatia, the Bible confirms, they were STOPPED by the Holy Spirit from preaching in those two places. (See Acts 16:6) What I want to remind believers is that though God has given us our own will, but if you also allow Him to lead and guide your path, He will make sure and do everything possible for you to get married to the right person in order that you may enjoy a peaceful marriage life in order to have peace of mind to serve Him better.

Now consider these passages which buttresses the point raised; *"FOR I KNOW THE PLANS I HAVE FOR YOU, DECLARES THE LORD, PLANS TO PROSPER YOU AND NOT TO HARM YOU, PLANS TO GIVE YOU HOPE AND A FUTURE"*. Jer.29:11. "**FOR MY WAYS ARE NOT YOUR WAYS AND MY THOUGHT NOT YOUR THOUGHT**". Isaiah 55:8. *"MANY ARE THE PLANS IN A MAN'S HEART, BUT IT IS THE LORD'S PURPOSE THAT PREVAILS"*. Prov.19:21. These passages show us believers who are being led by the Spirit of God that we should learn to submit ourselves to the direction of God, and He will not let us down, because the scriptures say; *"EVERY GOOD AND PERFECT GIFT*

IS FROM ABOVE, COMING DOWN FROM THE FATHER OF THE HEAVENLY LIGHTS, WHO DOES NOT CHANGE LIKE SHIFTING SHADOWS". James 1:16-17.

Frankly, you may not know why you lost your previous job, or you may not understand why you left that town, city or country for another. You may not understand why your trip failed, or you may not understand why you find yourself in this or that church. You may not understand the reason why you find yourself in this or that situation. There may be a lesson in it for you, so open your eyes and ears and make yourself available for God to connect you to the right marriage partner. He may like to use you to fulfill His promise He has made with His servant. Therefore, it may be helpful to know that the earlier you avail yourself the easier it will be to avert problems. Some believers are able to say plainly, I do not want to marry anyone who has given birth before, or anyone who comes from this or that tribe or this country or that country. These believers should advise themselves that if they know the gift of God, and the one He is giving you, they would have made themselves available long time. (See John 4:10)

Biblical example is Boaz who became a genealogy of Jesus Christ when he accepted to marry Ruth, the Moabite woman. The book of Ruth will tell you how Boaz gathered courage to marry Ruth who was not from Israel but a Moabite, and that bold step he took brought him into the ancestry of Jesus Christ, the Savior. On the other hand, if Ruth had stayed in her country and did not come with Naomi, she would have not joined this respectable genealogy of the Messiah—Jesus Christ. For your record, Boaz and Ruth were the great-grand children of David, the king.

Therefore, I urge spinsters and bachelors in the Lord to accept God's choice for that will be the best for them as far as marriage is concern. Always meditate on these texts; Jer.6:16, 29:11, Isaiah 55:8-12, Prov.19:21 James 1:16-17, **JEREMIAH 1:12.**

DREAM AND VISION

We have seen two ways of how God gives suitable partners, the third one is DREAM AND VISION which should have been the easiest and simplest way for believers to identify their suitable partners, but the devil has dominated this area and he is directing and misleading carnal believers to the wrong partners.

As Christians we are not to despise dreams and visions, but we are to prove all things. Of course, God revealed an important message to Nebuchadnezzar in dream. (See Dan.2:1-49, 3:1-30, 4:1-37) Daniel also dreamed and again had a vision. (See Dan.7:1-28, 8:1-27, 10:1-21) Again, God spoke to Joseph and Pharaoh in a dream and the dreams were fulfilled. (See Gen.37:1-11, 40:1-23, 41:1-57, 50:15-18). All these Bible references proof and confirm the point that God reveals certain things to us in dreams and visions, so you must be watchful if you are praying about your marriage partner.

However, you must be very careful and do not rely wholly on a dream or vision because it is not all dreams and visions which come from God. The devil is a very cunning and deceitful creature that is always at work to make things difficult for believers. He and his accomplices have led many people astray when they were choosing their spouses.

A certain brother came to inform me about the dream he had about a lady when he was praying for his future marriage. He said, he saw a lady sitting under a tree in the dream, and a voice came, this is your wife! He approached and had a conversation with her. When he woke up, he went to the place he saw the lady, fortunately for him, he found that nice pretty lady he saw in the dream at that same place. He started talking to her and she seemed to be the one God had chosen for him, because she was very nice and it seemed she had some potential in her that could make her a good wife.

I asked him if that lady was a Christian. He said 'no, but I will convert her later after the proposal'. In fact, he had already developed love for her which made it difficult for me to say anything that could discourage him. I could not stop him from planning for that dangerous marriage. However I tried my best to draw his attention to the word of God concerning such incidences in Christianity. We read the following two Bible passages; "**DO NOT BE YOKED TOGETHER WITH UNBELIEVER. FOR WHAT DO RIGHTEOUNESS AND WICKEDNESS HAVE IN COMMON?**" 2Cor.6:14. *"YOU ADULTEROUS PEOPLE, DON'T YOU KNOW THAT FRIENDSHIP WITH THE WORLD IS HATRED*

TOWARDS GOD? ANYONE WHO CHOOSES TO BE A FRIEND OF THE WORLD BECOMES AN ENEMY OF GOD". James 4:4.

These passages really helped him after we discussed about them. He was appreciative of the fact that had he not confided in me, he would have been put into a big trouble. Believers, be watchful! Because our enemy; the devil has not given up chasing after us. They are working hard to cause our downfall so that we may join them in their rebellion. As believers, in order that we will not join them in their rebellion against God, we must try to avoid anything that makes God unhappy about us. One of these things is DIVORCE! (See Mal.2:14-16). Therefore, believers especially the ladies, who always depend on seeing their partners in dreams or visions, must advise themselves with this lesson. (See Prov.4:16, 2 Cor.2:11, 1 Peter 5:8.)

Dreams and visions may be the simplest way for believers to see their future spouses, but Satan is also using this same method to deceive many believers to get married to the wrong partners. On the other hand, some of these dreams may also come from our own thinking and lust. *"AS A DREAM COMES WHEN THERE ARE MANY CARES, SO THE SPEECH OF A FOOL WHEN THERE ARE MANY WORDS".* Eccl. 5:3.

Whenever anyone has a dream concerning his marriage partner or whatever it is, try as much as possible to compare it to the word of God, and you may see if it comes from God, the devil or your own lust—personal desire and expectations. This is one of the reasons we are being admonished to worship God in Spirit and in truth. This will help us identify good dreams from God, and bad dreams form the devil. (See John 4:23-24, Heb.5:13-14).

Finally, you must be watchful if you are praying to get a suitable partner to marry, because God can give you a suitable partner though any of these directions we have studied. Either in a recommendation, circumstance, dream or vision, but if your friends got their spouses through a dream, you may also get yours through a recommendation. It all depends on God's will for you, but in all it is the same Lord who gives good and perfect partners to all who love Him. (John 14:21, James 1:16-17).

CHAPTER 12

PRACTICAL CHRISTIAN MARRIAGE

The theme for this chapter must be well understood, because there are different kinds of marriages on the earth. Christians are marrying as well as Muslims, pagans, unbelievers and other religions are also marrying. But in this chapter, we are considering how God, the institutor of marriage wants or expects His chosen ones to behave in their marriage. We are considering how He expects men to live with their wives, and how women should also live with their husbands. As you read on you may find some things difficult and controversial or debatable because of how you understand marriage. The way Africans understand and practice marriage is different from other parts of the world. But this subject is called "PRACTICAL CHRISTIANS' MARRIAGE". Practical here means the real marriage of believers; the original state of marriage God instituted which has a condition attached.

Let's first examine how God instituted the first marriage in the Garden of Eden. *"THE LORD GOD SAID, IT IS NOT GOOD FOR THE MAN TO BE ALONE. I WILL MAKE A HELPER SUITABLE FOR HIM. SO THE LORD GOD CAUSED THE MAN TO FALL INTO DEEP SLEEP, AND WHILE HE WAS SLEEPING, HE TOOK ONE OF THE MAN'S RIB AND CLOSED UP THE PLACE WITH A FLESH. THEN THE LORD GOD MADE A WOMAN FROM THE RIB HE HAD TAKEN OUT OF THE MAN, AND HE BROUGHT HER TO THE MAN. THE MAN SAID, THIS IS NOW BONE OF MY BONES AND FLESH*

OF MY FLESH, SHE SHALL BE CALLED WOMAN, FOR SHE WAS TAKEN OUT OF MAN. FOR THIS REASON A MAN WILL ***LEAVE*** *HIS FATHER AND MOTHER AND* ***BE UNITED*** *TO HIS WIFE, AND THEY SHALL* ***BECOME ONE FLESH****. THE MAN AND HIS WIFE WERE BOTH NAKED, AND THEY FELT NO SHAME".* Gen.2:18-25.

The above passage you just read shows how God instituted marriage and the condition attached to it. The condition attached to it is not a law with an accompanying punishment should there be a violation, but it is 'A MUST DO PRACTICE' which makes every marriage successful. If you want your marriage to be successful, then you must apply it into your marriage. Almost everybody on the earth will enter into marriage, because the Lord God said it is not good for man to live alone, he needs a helper—marriage partner. (Gen.2:18) The scriptures confirm this; "TWO ARE BETTER THAN ONE". Eccl.4:9-12. Unfortunately, some people who could not practice its rules have experienced hardship in it, while others have even lost both their lives and salvation through marital problems. It depends on how couples understand it, and how they conduct themselves. If you follow God's instruction you will really enjoy, but if you fail or refuse to follow, then you will see the bad side of the world in marriage. The reason is that for instance, the one who invented a vehicle, made some rules of how it should be driven. We all know the driver must sit behind the steer and control the car with other rules in it to make sure there will be no problem. Now, nobody can say he is more experienced in driving so he can sit at the other side of the car and drive. Although he might be able to drive with some experience and magic, but at the end of the day, an accident is going to happen at all cost—because that is not the rules in driving. Most of the accidents on our roads everyday are being caused by some drivers who ignore the rules in driving.

Similarly any couple who wants to have real enjoyment on marriage must make it their aim to follow its rules or direction. Then, what does God want us to do in our marriages to make it successful? The answer to this question can be found in the passage we read from Genesis 2:18-25. After God gave the woman to the man, He gave them three conditions attached to it that could make it beautiful and pleasant to enjoy by both of them. Therefore, if anyone fails to apply these three things, then definitely, problems will automatically come into such a marriage. But if these three things are applied correctly, then they will enjoy a very good marriage life.

So stay focus as you keep reading these conditions and apply it to your marriage.

LEAVING: "For this reason a man will **leave** his father and mother and . . ." Gen.2:24. According to the passage, immediately a man plans to marry, the first thing he must do is to leave his parent because anyone who is ready to settle down with a woman must be able to take care of himself and the wife.

I understand leaving as giving a space. The way you were very close to your parent must be continued but with some space this time bearing in mind that someone has joined you. You were one when you were with your parent but now you are two. Sometime ago you used to spend much time on the phone talking and laughing with your mother, but now your spouse wants your attention. If your spouse may want to speak to you and you are on the phone spending a long time talking to your mom, your spouse can be frustrated and may be inwardly annoyed. This can gradually become a big problem in the very near future if you keep doing this. You must leave your mom, and talk to your spouse—better-half! If you want your marriage to be as successful as God arranged it, then if you are with your mother or father on the phone, the condition attached to marriage demands that you LEAVE your parents and pay attention to your spouse until his or her need is addressed before you can continue with them.

Yes, I told you some things in this lesson can confuse you or it will be difficult to accept because of your understanding and how you are practicing marriage. This issue has caused lot of problems for some couples and has even destroyed some marriages. It is quite unfortunate for a husband to return home from work only to find his wife on the phone talking to her parents without recognizing his presence. The condition attached to marriage which can make it beautiful and pleasant demands that when your spouse arrives home, whoever you are talking to must be stopped and attention given to him or her before continuing with the phone conversation. Is that right? Yes! Even if you are talking to your pastor, a bishop or General overseer or even to Mr. President, kindly let him hold on and pay attention to your spouse, then come back and continue with your conversation.

God is superior or greater than anybody on the earth, so you must be obedient to Him more than anyone on earth. But because of VAIN GLORY, some spouses ignore His instruction in marriage, and the result is divorce—GREAT REBELLION! (Mal.2:14-16)

However, this condition in marriage does not apply to parent alone. It also affects everybody and everything such as work. Of course, work is causing much problem in marriages especially businessmen and women. Because of business, some spouses abandon their spouses and give all their attention to their businesses and the result sometimes is adultery. I hope you understand what I mean? Back home in Africa, we hear some wives sleep with their drivers, gardeners, men servants and husband's employees because the husband is a very busy person traveling from one city or country to another doing BUSINESS. In his absence, the gardener enjoys himself doing his job for him as a husband. As a husband in Christ, you must LEAVE your business in order to pay attention to your beautiful wife you have cared so much for and the good Lord will be pleased with you.

Sadly, we also hear that some mighty men of God rather love the kingdom business even more than their beautiful wives. These ministers travel from one place to another ministering powerfully. When they come home, the little time they may have for their wives is also used for counseling and other activities. When this becomes too unbearable, it ends up in either adultery or divorce. Of course, it's good to be zealous for the work of the Lord, but the Lord Himself who arranged marriage and attached a condition to it, demands that you to give a little SPACE to your ministry and pay attention to your beautiful wife and the Lord will be pleased with you and your ministry.

Also it is a sad to see some spouses backing their mothers, sisters or some other people against their spouses when there are conflicts between them. Even if your spouse is wrong, you don't have to do that—backing your mom against your spouse! Don't do that again if you want to maintain the happiness in your marriage. On the other hand, if your parents or any family member comes to visit you, let them know the house does not belong to you alone, even if you built or bought it before marriage. Therefore, they must behave well and not think I have come to my son, daughter or nephew's house, so I can do what I want. If they were doing those things when you were single, let them know they do not have that chance anymore—Let them know!

Some people cannot enjoy the happiness in marriage because they cannot LEAVE their family after getting married. But bear in mind that whenever leaving is not working in marriage, there may be a problem at all cost, because God attached it to make it successful. Surely, you cannot change what God has arranged, so try as much as possible to LEAVE your people when you get married.

All that I want mothers, fathers, uncles, brothers, sisters, family and friends to know is that if they want their sons, daughters or nephews to enjoy good and peaceful marriage life, then they should let them LEAVE when they get married, and the Good Lord will be pleased you! In fact, I am not saying they should not visit or stay with them or come to them for any help when the need arises, BUT I AM TALKING ABOUT THE INQUISITIVE AND INQUISITION! You may visit your children for a good reason, but if it happens to be a disturbances to their beautiful marriage, then the word of God must apply, and you must LEAVE!

BE UNITED—CLEAVING: God expects couples to leave everything and **be united** to their spouses. This also means the couple should be closest to each other than any other thing or person. But some believers have forgotten this rule in marriage, and have cleaved to their business and other things and people rather than their spouses. Some husbands may go to work early in the morning and LEAVE their wives alone until very late in the night before returning home. When the wife complains and wants the husband to do something about it, these husbands make excuses that it is the business that fend for their needs.

It may be true but God who supplies all our needs through these businesses demands the husband must **leave** that business in order to **CLEAVE** to their wives. This rule also applies to wives who must cleave to their husbands rather than any other thing, even their babies should not be an excuse just as men should not use their businesses which feeds the whole family as excuse. This will prevent Satan from outwitting you and causing any problem like divorce. (See 2Cor.2:11).

ONE FLESH: God expects couples to **LEAVE** everything including their parent and **CLEAVE** to their spouses and **BECOME ONE FLESH.** The two people becoming ONE FLESH means TOGETHERNESS between the couples. In marriage, God expects couples to be UNITED and become ONE FLESH by sharing or doing everything together. Whatever belongs to the husband belongs to the wife. Marriage demands couples to stay and live together at one place. Ideally, the couple should do everything possible to avoid staying apart. You are not supposed to stay in a different town, city, country nor continent so that the devil may not utilize that opportunity to lure any of you into sin such as adultery. Also try as much as possible to live and sleep together in one house or apartment and in one or the same room because you are one not two! (See Eccl.4:9-12).

I told you earlier that because of your culture and tradition, this may be difficult for some people to practice, and some people cannot accept this teaching because of how they were trained. But what I received from God is what I'm giving to you, if you take them seriously and put them into practice, you will definitely enjoy in your marriage. On the contrary if it is rejected, then, problems will definitely arise in such a marriage.

Let me share my view of this question with you; when the devil visited Eve in the Garden of Eden, where was Adam? Do you believe if Adam was with his wife at that particular time, the devil could have succeeded in deceiving them? The recorder of this story made a thought provoking statement regarding the location of Adam during Eve's encounter with the devil. ***"SHE ALSO GAVE SOME TO HER HUSBAND, WHO WAS WITH HER, AND HE ATE IT".*** Gen.3:6. But I am strongly convinced Adam was going around the Garden because he was the care-taker who was supposed to visit the Garden and to make sure everything was going on well before God would visit them. Perhaps he returned to see them talking when the wife had already eaten it. She gave him some and he also ate out of LOVE.

Although Adam knew it was an act of disobedience to eat that fruit, he ate all the same because of love. "***LOVE COVERS OVER A MULTITUDE OF SINS***". 1 Peter 4:8. "***AND ADAM WAS NOT THE ONE DECEIVED; IT WAS THE WOMAN WHO WAS DECEIVED AND BECAME A SINNER".*** 1 Tim.2:14. The devil planned very well before he took that step which eventually subdued them. He might have been around and was monitoring them, and when he found out that the man (Adam) had left his wife to another place, he quickly came in there to deceive her, knowing very well he would succeed.

In view of this, couple who stay apart—different places should advise themselves with this lesson. Some men can be faithful to their wives without committing adultery, but if for any reason they stay apart, only few can remain faithful to their wives and God. The same thing applies to the women, only few of them can remain faithful to their husbands and God. Although, some find it easy to commit such sin even if their beautiful wives and handsome husbands are with them, but I am talking about those who are worshipping God faithfully as the Father seeks. (See John 4:23-24.) Therefore, Christians who understand God's mind for instituted marriage should do well to stay together and do everything together in order that Satan may not tempt them with sin. (2Cor.2:11)

Finally, the couple should share these things together such as; joy, suffering, poverty, wealth, health, feeling, failure, success, shame and glory. You must feel what your spouse feels, if your spouse is hurting or in pains, do not just relax, but pay attention to him or her and find solutions together to that problem. Some men mistakenly insult and join their mothers and sisters to disturb their wives for their inability to have children. Because of such cases, I always advise young ladies to consult God properly before they choose their spouses. The Omniscient God alone is the One who knows the man who can bear your suffering and shame with you in times of troubles and have patience for you. The one who can pray earnestly with you for the problems you are going through, but not the one who can BETRAY you at the time of difficulties. The one who can understand that you WOMEN are eager to handle babies and be mothers more than they who want to be fathers. Therefore, if you are choosing your marriage partners, never look at the present appearance and situation, but look ahead and think of the future—that in case of difficulties, can this man be patience with me? In case I'm faced with barrenness, can this man stand firm behind me if my in-laws are coming with disturbances? Spinsters and bachelors in the Lord should consider all these factors before they choose their spouses, in order that they will not fall into the hand of the devil. Always bear in mind that in every successful marriage where Satan cannot have any role to play, there should be a LEAVING, CLEAVING AND BECOMING ONE FLESH. Therefore, Christian couples should understand that without these three things, marriage cannot be successful—so put them into practice and avoid being APART!

CHAPTER 13

A SUITABLE HELPER

"THE LORD GOD SAID, IT IS NOT GOOD FOR THE MAN TO BE ALONE. ***I WILL MAKE A HELPER SUITABLE FOR HIM****. NOW THE LORD HAD FORMED OUT OF THE GROUND ALL THE WILD ANIMALS AND ALL THE BIRDS IN THE SKY. HE BROUGHT THEM TO THE MAN TO SEE WHAT HE WOULD NAME THEM; AND WHATEVER THE MAN CALLED EACH LIVING CREATURE, THAT WAS ITS NAME. SO THE MAN GAVE NAMES TO ALL THE LIVESTOCK, THE BIRDS IN THE SKY AND ALL THE WILD ANIMALS. BUT FOR ADAM,* ***NO SUITABLE HELPER*** *WAS FOUND. SO THE LORD GOD CAUSED THE MAN TO FALL INTO DEEP A SLEEP; AND WHILE HE WAS SLEEPING, HE TOOK ONE OF THE MAN'S RIBS AND THEN CLOSED UP THE PLACE WITH FLESH. THEN THE LORD GOD MADE A WOMAN FROM THE RIB HE HAD TAKEN OUT OF THE MAN, AND HE BROUGHT HER TO THE MAN"*. Gen.2:18-22.

This long passage shows women were purposely created as SUITABLE HELPERS for men. (1Cor.11:9) Before a woman was created, man was making life already by himself and he was lonely, so God immediately noticed and acted on it before something bad could happen to him. Initially and originally, God needed only man to take care of his creation, but when He later found out that he may not be able to survive, He then planned for the creation of the woman purposely to be a great helper to him. (See Gen.2:18-25, 1 Cor.11:7-9)

Some time past, some people were having a hot debate that it was Adam who first asked God why He created everything in twos—male and female, but not him, and God said you have asked for trouble. I explained to them that this is not biblical but it is coming from devil to make them perceive women as troublesome. Unfortunately, some women are also behaving as troublesome indeed! Certainly God declares women as HELPERS for men but not TROUBLESOME. They were not created to trouble men, but to fit in as SUITABLE HELPERS!

Therefore, any woman who has changed her original nature as a SUITABLE HELPER and is now seen as a torn in the flesh—TROUBLESOME to a man, **that woman will appear before the judgment seat of God and respond to that**. (See 2 Cor.5:10) The man had started living by himself and God realized he needed a perfect helper but not just a helper—somebody who can fit in perfectly. If it was not that important and special reason, the Lord would have created another man to assist Adam in the Garden. The reason God described the woman as a HELPER is because of her work at home.

When we consider bachelors in the rural areas especially in Africa, they wake up from bed, sweep and clean their room, fetch water with a bucket from a distant river or tap, wash their clothes and cook their food and then go to work. All these chores will make him tired and weak, and can even shorten his life if God did not bring women into his life. This is one of the reasons God created women and called them HELPER in the lives of men, because some of the household responsibilities which men find them difficult are easy for women. For this reason, God expects every woman to understand she is a HELPER on this earth in the life of a man.

However, men should understand properly the duty and the description of the name given to women. Considering the behavior and attitude of some men and husbands, it shows they misinterpret or misunderstand the word HELPER. Frankly, this word HELPER does not mean or not represent SPECIAL ASSISTANCES OR SECRETARIES as we see in managers' offices. No! Your wife cannot be your special assistance, not at all! She is your SUITABLE HELPER—which means you need her to survive, that is why the scriptures say; "*HE WHO FINDS WIFE FINDS WHAT IS GOOD AND RECEIVES FAVOR FROM THE LORD*". Prov.18:22.

When men understand what their wives mean to them, they will treat them with due respect.

Women should also understand God's mind for creating them on this earth. You are all helpers of men. You have been created to help your husbands to make life easier for them. That is why we have a saying that; *"BEHIND EVERY SUCCESSFUL MAN, THERE IS A WOMAN".* Of course, this is true because even some ministers of God who are doing well in the ministry have good and hardworking women backing them at home. Therefore, women should understand they are men's helpers, so if your husband's work is not doing well, and for some time now you have not given him any food to eat, then you have failed the duty which God created you to perform on this earth.

Whenever a man proposes love to a woman, he means come into his life as a helper. Some men propose in this way; '**please will you be my wife?**' and it means, '**can you be my helper?**' Because every man needs a helper, so it is normal for a man to ask a woman to become his helper which also termed as 'better-half'. Thus, if you accept his proposal, it means you have accepted to be his helper in every way and in everything, but not his 'special assistance'.

If you know you cannot be his helper, find a polite way to refuse that proposal, but do not try to accept it because you need a husband or he is rich. If you accept to marry a man without the intention to help him but to gain from him, it is a wrong motive from the devil to destroy your fellowship with God. By this, men also in the Lord must pray earnestly to the Lord to guide them choose women who are ready to help them to make life easier for them.

On the other hand, women who have no intentions of becoming helpers for men should do well to avoid getting married. That is better than getting married and may not perform your duty as a suitable helper. I know a lady who finds it difficult to be a helper to a man. She has rented a room by herself and has placed everything in it to make it comfortable for her in order that she may not lack anything that may cause her to accept any proposal for marriage. In Africa, women know they will marry and move in with their husbands. So they do not used to do what this lady did by renting a nice place for herself. This shows she meant what she said, and it is better for her to STAY PUT than to marry and cannot perform her duty as suitable helper in the life of a man. (See 1 Cor.7:25-28) In this case, if any woman also knows for any reason she may not be able to be a helper in marriage to a man, please STAY OFF on the way of marriage in order not to cause problem to yourself and that unfortunate man, because marriage without a woman's intention to help the man cannot be a successful marriage.

Fathers and mothers who use force to choose partners for their sons and daughters should stop and understand that, if your children do not genuinely accept the people you choose or recommend for them, all your efforts of helping will rather destroy their marriage. Your duty as a parent in Christ is to train them in the fears of God and support them in prayers and leave the rest to them and God. No matter how far you have raised your daughters in life, either in education or financially, they are all helpers of men in marriage, and they must be allowed to choose anyone they know they can help as you (wives) were allowed to choose your own husbands when you were young ladies. If all of us understand God's intention for instituting marriage and what He is expecting from us, then Satan will have no chance in our marriages. Therefore, all of us should understand that women are the HELPERS OF MEN in every way in their lives through marriage. (See Gen.2:18, Prov.30:19.)

CHAPTER 14

THE RESPONSIBILITY OF HUSBAND AND WIFE IN MARRIAGE

We are still trying to sort out certain things the devil uses to lure believers into rebelling against God; thus giving him an opportunity in the life of the transgressors to subdue them. As previously mentioned, believers have been ENGRAVED in the hands of Almighty God, making it impossible for the devil to subdue us (See Isaiah 49:14-17, Jer.20:11, Psalm 31:20, Rom.8:31, Heb.13:6). Although we have great protection from Almighty God, the devil has not given up his pursuit. He has sent out his accomplices to compel believers to get themselves out from this great protection of God (See Prov.4:16, 1 Peter 5:8).

In this chapter, we are considering one of the things Satan uses to get many believers to rebel against God. God said, "***I HATE DIVORCE***". Mal.2:16. Therefore, believers must try as much as possible to avoid anything which may lead to divorce. The devil entices believers to do what God hates, causing them to deviate from God's discipline that he may grab the erring believer into destruction with him. This is the very reason the Lord has laid on my heart to share with you how we may know his devices in order to avoid the devil's traps. (See 2 Cor.2:11)

Now, "what is the responsibility of a husband and wife in marriage?" Unfortunately, when I put forth this question to couples who usually quarrel, they usually answer it incorrectly. The old fashioned reply is that the wife is responsible for washing, cooking, cleaning, and all the domestic chores; whereas the husband's responsibility is to provide the finances by which he may provide shelter, food, education and pay all the bills and debts of the family. Briefly, the wife's duty is to take care of the house, and the husband's is to financially provide for the family. In fact, adopting this marriage system is causing great harm to many marriages. If you understand your duties in marriage in this way, the devil surely has a chance in to take away your happiness, which may eventually lead to divorce—which is what we are trying to avoid.

The reason this understanding causes problems in marriage is that some husbands do nothing at home and leave the entire burden on their wives; eventually the woman becomes tired of the burden and this becomes a reason to conflict. Some men do not know how to cook food and also do not like to eat out, so if for one reason or another the woman is unable to cook and asks the husband to do so, he may think of it as disrespectful; and this sometimes starts quarrels. In some African customs and traditions, the wife dares not tell her husband to sweep or wash clothes. In fact, these petty things cause conflicts and quarrels in marriage. In the same way, a wife may also find it difficult if her husband has a bad job or low income when she earns more if they are governed by this mindset.

There was once an elder of a church who lost his job later after getting married. His wife did not give him food for more than two years. This wife believed that it was up to her husband to fend for the family and not her. Do you now realize how the problem develops? By the time I heard this story, the elder was planning for a DIVORCE, and by so doing, breaking God's command. It is not biblical to live by this understanding of the roles of a husband and wife; these are but customs and traditions of many cultures in the world. Now let's identify from scripture what the true responsibilities of the husband and wife are in marriage.

THE RESPONSIBILITY OF WIVES;

*"**WIVES, SUBMIT** TO YOUR HUSBANDS AS TO THE LORD. FOR THE HUSBAND IS THE HEAD OF THE WIFE AS CHRIST IS THE HEAD OF THE CHURCH, HIS BODY, OF WHICH HE IS THE SAVIOR. NOW AS THE CHURCH SUBMITS TO CHRIST,*

SO ALSO ***WIVES*** *SHOULD* ***SUBMIT*** *TO THEIR HUSBANDS IN EVERYTHING*". Eph.5:22-24.

As a wife in the Lord, your responsibility in marriage is **SUBMISSION!** That is to submit to your husband and it means HUMILITY—to humble yourself before your husband. If a wife understands this as her responsibility, she is now going to think of the deeper meaning and the implications of submission which may include household chores. In this way the last sentence of the passage we previously mentioned will be fulfilled which states: '*Wives* ***SHOULD*** *submit to their husbands in EVERYTHING'*. Eph.5:24.

Therefore, the wife who fears God and understands the word and verb SUBMISSION and SUBMIT respectively, will not sit down idle while her husband who is her head is washing his clothes, sweeping the room, or doing some other domestic task. All these household chores are not mentioned as your duty, but it's good in the sight of God to do it not as your task but as HELP, because you are helpers of men in marriage. Remember I previously mentioned that some of things which men find difficult to do are easier for you; it is God who created you in this way. So Apostle Paul encouraged Titus to teach older women to train the younger ones who have just started on their journey in marriage to humble themselves before their husbands so that no-one will MALIGN the word of God. (See Titus 2:3-5)

Apostle Peter also added his voice to this and said: if wives are able to submit to their husbands, the unbelievers may be won over into Christ without a word, but by their behaviors. (See 1 Peter 3:1-2) He continued that; "*YOUR BEAUTY SHOULD NOT COME FROM OUTWARD ADORNMENT SUCH AS BRAIDED HAIR AND THE WEARING OF THE GOLD JEWELLERY AND FINE CLOTHES. INSTEAD, IT SHOULD BE THAT OF YOUR* ***INNERSELF,*** *THE UNFADING BEAUTY OF A GENTLE AND QUIET SPIRIT, WHICH IS OF GREAT WORTH IN GOD'S SIGHT. FOR THIS IS THE WAY THE HOLY WOMEN OF THE PAST WHO PUT THEIR HOPE IN GOD USED TO MAKE THEMSELVES BEAUTY.* ***THEY WERE SUBMISSIVE TO THEIR OWN HUSBANDS*** *LIKE SARAH, WHO OBEYED ABRAHAM AND CALLED HIM HER MASTER. YOU ARE HER DAUGHTERS IF YOU*

DO WHAT IS RIGHT AND DO NOT GIVE WAY TO FEAR". 1 Peter 3:3-6.

Wives in the Lord! This is your responsibility in marriage and understanding this will help you to do better than you are doing now, as we consider the PRACTICAL CHRISTIAN MARRIAGE. Also remember that no matter how much you have been raised up in life, either in education, financially or anything else, if your HOPE is in the Lord, then learn to submit to your OWN husbands to whom you have accepted to be their suitable helpers. Therefore, "***WIVES, SUBMIT TO YOUR HUSBANDS, AS IT IS FITTING IN THE LORD".*** Col.3:18.

THE RESPONSIBILITY OF HUSBANDS IN MARRIAGE

The responsibility of the husband is LOVE. *"HUSBANDS, **LOVE** YOUR WIVES JUST AS CHRIST LOVED THE CHURCH AND GAVE HIMSELF UP FOR HER, TO MAKE HER HOLY, CLEANSING HER BY THE WASHING WITH WATER THROUGH THE WORD AND TO PRESENT HER TO HIMSELF AS RADIANT CHURCH, WITHOUT STAIN OR WRINKLE OR ANY OTHER BLEMISH, BUT HOLY AND BLAMELESS. IN THE SAME WAY, HUSBANDS OUGHT TO **LOVE** THEIR WIVES AS THEIR OWN **BODIES**. HE WHO **LOVES** HIS WIFE LOVES HIMSELF".* Eph.5:25-28.

This passage shows the husband's responsibility in marriage is love. Just as the wife should seek the deeper and practical meanings of submission, the husband ought to seek the deeper and practical meanings of loving his wife.

How do you show love to your wife? The husband who loves his wife protects, cherishes, honors and provides for her needs. All these must be done from the pure heart as if you were doing it for yourself. If the husband understands his responsibility in this way, the devil may not have a chance to cause a misunderstanding in that marriage.

A husband cannot truthfully claim he loves his wife if she is very busy doing all the household chores while he is free from work just reading news papers, books or Bible or even playing. I reminded you earlier that you were doing these things by yourself before God brought her to help reduce your load. For this reason, do not leave everything to her saying you are a man and therefore she must do all these as her duty.

The reason husbands are advised to feed and care for their wives is that Apostle Paul illustrated that he who loves his wife loves himself, and no one has ever hated his own body, but he feeds and cares for it, just as Christ does for the church. (See Eph.5:28-30). I know for sure anyone who is thirsty will do everything possible to get water to drink to be free from thirst. If you are hungry, you will try as much as possible to get some food to eat to satisfy your stomach. So the passage simply means apply the same conditions to your wife who is in fact a part of you.

When Apostle Peter added his voice, he said; *"HUSBANDS, IN THE SAME WAY BE CONSIDERATE AS YOU LIVE WITH YOUR WIVES, AND TREAT THEM WITH **RESPECT** AS THE WEAKER PARTNER AS HEIRS WITH YOU OF THE GRACIOUS GIFT OF LIFE, SO THAT NOTHING WILL HINDER YOUR **PRAYERS**"* (See 1Peter 3:7). This passage also reveals a mystery here: if the husband fails to love and respect his wife, it can break up his fellowship with God and his prayers will not get to Him. The devil is aware of these scriptures, which is why he works hard to entice the husband to do what ought not to be done to his wife; which does not show love in the sight of God. The Lord expects you to give due respect to your wife who has been specially prepared to help you. Apostle Peter described her as the ***gracious gift*** from God to you.

Husband in the Lord! This is your responsibility in marriage. If you understand your responsibility in this way, it will help you to do better than what you are doing now and your prayers will go straight to God, because you love and respect your wife. Apostle Paul concluded this subject that; ***"LOVE YOUR WIVES AND DO NOT BE HARSH ON THEM"*** (See Col. 3:19).

CHAPTER 15

WHY DOES THE RIGHTEOUS SUFFER?

We have learned from chapter three that God disciplines believers who disobey and rebel against Him by causing them to encounter problems and suffering. However, there are some believers who fear and keep the word of God and yet face similar problems. So '*WHY DOES THE RIGHTEOUS ALSO SUFFER?*'

Biblically, there were some believers who kept the word of God and served Him respectfully with their whole heart, but they also went through a lot of suffering—DISGRACE AND HUMILIATION. Believers such as Abraham, Job, Joseph, Hannah, John the Baptist, Steven, Paul and many other who served God with due respect and humility also faced all kinds of suffering. Even Joseph who ran away from what an unbeliever may view as a 'Scholarship' from a highly respected and beautiful woman, ended up in prison. The Bible did not record in any chapter or verse that Hannah did something to provoke God to close her womb. Again, there was no report that Steven insulted the chief priest or a ruler that led him to being stoned to death.

Likewise, some believers have obeyed the word of God and kept themselves pure in order to enjoy the kindness of God (See Psalm 18:20-30, Rom.11:22) yet, these believers also encounter difficulties in life. This is what is called; '**THE TRIAL AND TEST OF BELIEVERS**'. *"IN ALL THIS YOU GREATLY REJOICE, THOUGH NOW FOR A LITTLE WHILE YOU*

MAY HAVE HAD TO ***SUFFER GRIEF IN ALL KINDS OF TRIALS***". 1 Peter 1:6. *"DO NOT BE AFRAID OF WHAT YOU ARE ABOUT TO* ***SUFFER****. I TELL YOU, THE DEVIL WILL PUT SOME OF YOU IN PRISON TO* ***TEST*** *YOU, AND YOU WILL* ***SUFFER PERSECUTION FOR TEN DAYS****. BE FAITHFUL, EVEN TO THE POINT OF DEATH, AND I WILL GIVE YOU LIFE AS YOUR VICTOR'S CROWN"*. Rev.2:10.

I hope at the end of this lesson, you will not consider every believer who encounters difficulties in life is facing God's discipline because of sin. People, who professed to be believers, but have been hired by the devil to condemn believers in trials for various reasons, are making things extremely difficult for these believers. These sometimes results in some believers seeking solutions to their problems from ungodly sources, and usually end up losing their salvation which was bought with the precious blood of our Lord Jesus Christ. For this reason, I want us to consider the following reasons why righteous may also suffer. This will help the believer to be strong and stand firm in their faith and have hope that at the end of these trials, we are going to receive the VICTOR'S CROWN. (See Rev.2:10)

WHY DOES A RIGHTEOUS ALSO SUFFER?

1. The trials and suffering help believers to commit and submit themselves to God. *"GOD OPPOSES THE PROUD BUT SHOWS FAVOR TO THE HUMBLE AND OPPRESSED.* ***SUBMIT YOURSELVES****, THEN, TO GOD. RISIST THE DEVIL AND HE WILL FLEE FROM YOU. HUMBLE YOURSELVES BEFORE THE LORD, AND HE WILL LIFT YOU UP"* (James 4:6, 7, 10). ***"SO THEN, THOSE WHO SUFFER ACCORDING TO THE WILL OF GOD SHOULD COMMIT THEMSELVES TO THEIR FAITHFUL CREATOR AND CONTINUE TO DO GOOD".*** 1 Peter 4:19.

According to both passages, we see that some believers ought to go through some sufferings in order to learn how to commit and submit themselves to God. Many believers who claim to serve God do not rely on God but on themselves. They believe they will do well in life by their own effort, and this is a result of pride.

When a prayer program is organized, it's hard to see these people involved in it, simply because they do not have any problem. Many people suppose that those who attend prayer meetings and evening services are those who have some kind of problem. In fact, it is hard for these believers to fast and wait on God. (See Ezra 8:21, Isaiah 58:1-5) God may let such a believer experience suffering to cause the believer to become humble toward God in fasting. Sometimes this will cause them to visit prayer centers and the leaders of the centers may advise them to fast for a certain period.

In fact, this kind of suffering has caused some believers to become as effective as they are today. They may have faced a couple of problems in the past which caused them to seek the help of God, and have since then devoted themselves more appropriately to the service of the Lord. Therefore, believers who suffer according to the will of God should **COMMIT AND SUBMIT** themselves to their faithful Creator and continue to serve Him faithfully. 1 Peter 4:19.

2. Trials and sufferings help to assert those who are really children of God. *"SEE HOW GREAT LOVE THE FATHER HAS LAVISHED ON US,* ***THAT WE SHOULD BE CALLED THE CHILDREN OF GOD!*** *AND THAT IS WHAT WE ARE!"* **1John 3:1.** *"NOW IF WE ARE CHILDREN, THEN WE ARE HEIRS—HEIRS OF GOD AND CO-HEIRS WITH CHRIST,* ***IF INDEED WE SHARE IN HIS SUFFERING*** *IN ORDER THAT WE MAY ALSO SHARE IN HIS GLORY*—HALELUJAH!" Rom.8:17.

What an interesting passage this is. In many cases, some believers engage in great arguments and hot debates about who a child of God is. In fact, I do not answer this question for anyone, I answer only for myself. When someone joins the church and is baptized, we understand he is being born again and has become a new creation. If he truly converted to Christ Jesus, then he is a part of Christ Jesus as the Son of God and also shares in the privileges of Christ. But to assert this as true conversion, that so-called Christian has to go through some trials and suffering to identify his conversion as genuine.

As a matter of fact, God knows those who are genuinely converted and are His children (See 2 Tim.2:19), but going through these trials and suffering brings an end to all arguments. This is because, when a believer goes through trials, it is there that we see whether or not such a person has really converted into the image of Christ. (See Eph.4:20-24, Gen.1:26-27)

The first two passages we read state that; *'consider how great love the Father has lavished on us THAT WE SHALL BE CALLED THE CHILDREN OF GOD! AND THAT IS WHAT WE ARE!'* 1 John 3:1. In fact, claiming to be a child of God is not difficult. It is as easy as saying "1-2-3." However, when the trial comes the real identity shows. The second passage made a good point that; *'If we are children, then, we are heirs of God and co-heirs with Christ, if indeed we share in His suffering in order that we may also share in His glory'.* Rom.8:17. This passage also shows you to prepare to be tried and suffer with Christ, in order to also share in His glory to be revealed. What is your reaction to this point? Are you ready to face some kind of suffering, or will you deny your faith and confession? I encourage you to face the suffering and share in His glory because; **"I CONSIDER THAT OUR PRESENT SUFFERINGS ARE NOT WORTH COMPARING WITH THE GLORY THAT WILL BE REVEALED IN US"** (Rom.8:18). Is that clear? This tells you that believers who are in all kinds of suffering and difficulty should not be ridiculed. As in the story of the rich man and Lazarus, we learn that the rich man used to ridicule Lazarus concerning his situation which was preparing him for the kingdom of God. (See Luke 16:19-31)

Some ministers of God have taken advantage of other believers' lack of knowledge in the scriptures and are confusing them by teaching that in Christianity no one is suppose to be poor. Granted; but poverty can be someone's trial and suffering, therefore, those who are in such a situation should be encouraged and not despised. If you tell a believer that Christianity doesn't include earthly poverty and yet such a person is faced with poverty as a trial, what do you think this person will be led to think about the situation?

When God gives anyone to the tempter, he knows from where to start. He will surely start from where you are afraid to face. Let's consider Job's case, he loved his children very much and did not want them to perish, so he used to sacrifice for their sins in order to have maximum protection from God. When the devil got a chance to test him, he quickly started right from killing all his children. When Job was crying, listen to what he said: *"WHAT **I FEARED** HAS COME UPON ME; WHAT **I DREADED***

HAS HAPPENED TO ME. I HAVE NO PEACE, NO QUIETNESS; I HAVE NO REST, BUT ONLY TURMOIL". Job 3:25-26. Is that clear? So ministers of God, if life is easy for you please take it easy with your members, else, they will be confused and allow the devil steal their minds and hearts from God which could eventually end them up in destruction. Therefore, those who are in the trials must be encouraged, not discouraged. Thank you for your understanding. Let's continue.

3. **It is a sign or assurance of salvation;** *"WHATEVER HAPPENS, AS CITIZENS OF HEAVEN LIVE IN A MANNER WORTHY OF THE GOSPEL OF CHRIST. THEN, WHETHER I COME AND SEE YOU OR ONLY HEAR ABOUT YOU IN MY ABSENCE, I WILL KNOW THAT YOU STAND FIRM IN ONE SPIRIT, STRIVING TOGETHER WITH ONE ACCORD FOR THE FAITH OF THE GOSPEL WITHOUT BEING FRIGHTENED IN ANYWAY BY THOSE* ***WHO OPPOSE YOU. THIS IS SIGN TO THEM THAT THEY WILL BE DESTROYED, BUT THAT YOU WILL BE SAVED—AND THAT BY GOD.*** *FOR IT HAS BEEN GRANTED TO YOU ON BEHALF OF CHRIST, NOT ONLY TO BELIEVE ON HIM,* ***BUT ALSO TO SUFFER FOR HIM****, SINCE YOU ARE GOING THROUGH THE SAME STRUGGLE YOU SAW I HAD, AND NOW HEAR THAT I STILL HAVE".* Phil.1:27-31.

If you understand this passage clearly, you will no longer be surprise if someone hates or opposes you. You will not let it troubles you if your boss does not like you. You no longer let it bothers you if your supervisor is persecuting you. If your colleagues oppose you for no good reason, I'm sure it will not bother you again because this is a SIGN that if they do not repent, they stand to be CONDEMNED AND DESTROYED, and it is a SIGN to you that your salvation is secured.

This issue is also happening within the church, but I'm sure you know the reason why someone hates you so much in the church. Some believers also encounter persecution from the leadership of the church, because of their gifts and function/ministry in the church. Sometime ago in one of my local assemblies, I was chosen to lead the Sunday morning Bible study (before the main service). By God's grace I did my best and it was very interested to the congregation. Through this study the church was revived and even the time for Sunday morning service improved, because it got to a point that nobody wanted to miss Bible study. Apart from this I was also involved in other leadership positions of the various groups in the church, such as prayer warriors and witness movement. I was also the only a member who used to be paired with the elders to preach at the church revival service and the main church program. I was happily doing all these with the intention to help build the church. (Eph.4:12)

Unfortunately, there was one elder who had influence on the others and including the presiding elder, who realized I was becoming popular and for that matter decided to act secretly. He influenced the presiding elder to change the Bible study to prayers before the commencement of the service. That prayer was given to be led by one deacon who was highly favored by that elder. Soon the congregation also reacted and things started turning for the worst. The attendance decreased at once and the few people who would usually come to church also began to come very late. I wondered what was happening, thinking they do not like prayers.

When the presiding elder realized what was happening, he called me outside the temple one day and started begging and pleading with me to forgive him and forget whatever had happened. I asked him to stop why he was asking for forgiveness and I let him know that I was aware that such things tend to happen in the church of God. I was not offended in anyway because they are the leaders in the church and at the end of the year, they would be accountable to the district pastor and his executive, so he could choose to do what he thought could help build the church; I had no part to play in that. I am only a servant of the Lord Jesus who is always ready to serve Him with the gifts He has bestowed on me to help build His church.

I continued to do my best at whatever task I was given to do. As a matter of fact, even if for any reason, I am not given opportunity to minister for a whole year, I would not to be bothered by it because as the scripture says; "*WE ARE GOD'S WORKMANSHIP, CREATED IN CHRIST JESUS, TO DO GOOD WORKS WHICH GOD PREPARED IN ADVANCE FOR US TO DO*". Eph.2:10. He then revealed what was going on among them; it is not that they did not like prayer, but they realized something had gone wrong, because the Bible Study which was discontinued was really helping them. I told the elder that I knew the one who was instigating these conflicts. Surprised, he thought one of the elders had disclosed the information to me. However, nobody had told me anything; I rather discerned what happened on the platform. I assured him of my readiness to serve the Lord and we teamed together again and did what God wanted us to do which caused the church get to the level God intended for it before I left them to another place.

Believers I do not become surprised when something like this happens at church; because I know these scriptures which confirm that: *"FOR CERTAIN INDIVIDUALS WHOSE CONDEMNATION WAS WRITTEN ABOUT LONG AGO HAVE* ***SECRETLY SLIPPED IN AMONG YOU****. THEY ARE UNGODLY PEOPLE, WHO PERVERT THE GRACE OF OUR GOD INTO A LICENSE OF IMMORALITY AND DENY JESUS CHRIST OUR ONLY SOVEREIGN AND LORD"* Jude 4.

Believers, when you have these passages in mind, you will not bother yourselves with whoever opposes you in the ministry, because God does that to show you the people who have professed to be Christians but aren't, and to give you a sign that your salvation is firmly secured. (See Phi.1:27-31)

4. **Trials and sufferings prepare believers for the kingdom of God.** When we as believers become conscious of the benefits we get from trials and suffering in our Christians lives, we will not talk too much about them but will face them in good faith. But at times, those who aren't experiencing any trials in our midst which make the situation difficult for the rest who are being prepared by these trials and sufferings to receive the kingdom of God. However, Apostle Paul strengthened and encouraged believers of the reason we face all these kinds of hardship in life. *"STRENGTHENING THE DISCIPLES AND ENCOURAGING THEM TO REMAIN TRUE TO THE FAITH,* ***'WE MUST GO THROUGH MANY HARDSHIPS TO ENTER THE KINGDOM OF GOD****".* Acts 14:22. If anyone has this in mind, that he will spend his/her eternity with God in his Kingdom, then that believer must be prepared to go through many kinds of sufferings and trials.

5. **Trials and sufferings help believers to become strong in the Lord.** *"AND THE GOD OF ALL GRACE, WHO CALLED YOU TO HIS ETERNAL GLORY IN CHRIST, AFTER YOU HAVE SUFFERED*

A LITTLE WHILE, WILL HIMSELF RESTORE YOU AND MAKE YOU ***STRONG, FIRM AND STEADFAST.*** *TO HIM BE THE POWER FOR EVER AND EVER".* 1Peter 5:10-11. As we have discussed in the first point, trials and sufferings have helped some believers to learn how to pray and fast, else they would have been powerless being without motivation to pray. But now we thank God for these trials and sufferings, some believers, including myself, are used to living in any situation without being bothered by what people say or think about them. I don't have time to listen to what people say because we have heard enough, but in all we have been able to stand for the Lord as the scriptures say; "*THE PEOPLE WHO KNOW THEIR GOD SHALL BE STRONG AND DO EXPLOIT*". Dan.11:32.

6. **Trials and sufferings are sign of godly life or discipleship.** *"IN FACT, EVERYONE WHO WANTS TO LIVE A GODLY LIFE IN CHRIST JESUS WILL BE PERSECUTED"***.** 2Tim.3:12. *"VERY TRULY I TELL YOU, YOU WILL WEEP AND MOURN WHILE THE WORLD REJOICES. YOU WILL GRIEVE, BUT YOUR GRIEF WILL TURN TO JOY. A WOMAN GIVING BIRTH TO A CHILD HAS PAIN BECAUSE HER TIME HAS COME; BUT WHEN HER BABY IS BORN SHE FORGETS THE ANGUISH BECAUSE OF HER JOY THAT A CHILD IS BORN INTO THE WORLD. SO WITH YOU: NOW IS YOUR TIME OF GRIEF, BUT I WILL SEE YOU AGAIN AND YOU WILL REJOICE, AND NO ONE WILL TAKE AWAY YOUR JOY"*. John 16:20-22.

"DEAR FRIENDS, DO NOT BE SURPRISED AT THE PAINFUL TRIALS YOU ARE GOING THROUGH AS THOUGH SOMETHING STRANGE WERE HAPPENING TO YOU. BUT REJOICE INASMUCH AS YOU PARTICIPATE IN THE SUFFERING OF CHRIST, SO THAT YOU MAY BE OVERJOYED WHEN HIS GLORY IS REVEALED. IF YOU ARE INSULTED BECAUSE OF THE NAME OF CHRIST, YOU ARE BLESSED, FOR THE SPIRIT OF GLORY AND OF GOD RESTS ON YOU. IF YOU SUFFER, IT SHOULD NOT BE AS MURDERER OR THIEF OR ANY OTHER KIND OF CRIMINAL, OR EVEN AS A MEDDLER. HOWEVER, IF YOU SUFFER AS A CHRISTIAN, DO NOT BE ASHAMED, BUT PRAISE GOD THAT YOU BEAR THAT NAME". 1 Peter 4:12-16.

When you consider these passages, they show us believers who are going through all kinds of hardship are not experiencing something STRANGE, implying that suffering is a part of Christianity. Therefore, believers who are in some kind of trial and suffering should advise themselves with these passages in order that the devil may not confuse and entice you to do what you ought not to do. At the end of it all, God's name will be glorified.

7. **Trials and suffering prepare the man of God for special assignments in the ministry.** *"IN ALL THIS YOU GREATLY REJOICE, THOUGH NOW FOR A LITTLE WHILE* ***YOU MAY HAVE HAD TO SUFFER GRIEF OF ALL KINDS OF TRIALS****. THESE HAVE COME SO THAT YOUR* ***FAITH****—OF GREATER WORTH THAN GOLD, WHICH PERISHES EVEN THOUGH REFINED BY FIRE—****MAY BE PROVED GENUINE*** *AND MAY RESULT IN PRAISE, GLORY AND HONOR WHEN CHRIST JESUS IS REVEALED"*. 1 Peter 1:6-7.

"CONSIDER IT PURE JOY, MY BROTHERS AND SISTERS, WHENEVER YOU FACE ***TRIALS OF MANY KINDS****, BECAUSE YOU KNOW THAT THE* ***TESTING OF YOUR FAITH*** *PRODUCES PERSEVERANCE. LET PERSEVERANCE FINISH ITS WORK SO THAT YOU MAY BE* ***MATURE AND COMPLETE****, NOT LACKING ANYTHING"*. James 1:2-4.

Some believers are interested in becoming anointed by God to minister powerfully, but they are afraid to go though hardship as the training and test of their faith as both passages explain clearly to us. Therefore, believers who are interested in becoming anointed by God for ministry must be well prepared to suffer in all kinds of trials, when they prove genuine and mature, then a special anointing will be poured on them.

At this juncture, I hope readers of this book have received some good points to understand why does a righteous suffer, the question which is bothering many believers have been answered, I hope you will not allow the devil to confuse you by causing you to wonder why you are going through these problems after being faithful to God. Obviously, the lesson has proved to you that those who serve God faithfully are not exempt from hardship. When they endure, they will be glorified when Christ Jesus is revealed. (See 1 Peter 4:12-16)

My dear readers, this ends this subject and the whole book. It is to give you more enlightenment about how Satan is able to subdue the children of God, how God Himself disciplines His children, and how to enjoy the fellowship of God, including many other important subjects. If you take these lessons seriously by practicing them, you will be able to conquer the devil, or if you let him entice you to give up your position, he may teach you bad lesson in life. Therefore, Always be aware of his schemes that he may not outwit you. (See 2Cor.2:11).

You may turn to the next page and read the questions asked by some believers which are answered respectively. This may be helpful to you.

CHAPTER 16

QUESTIONS AND ANSWERS

1. **QUESTION**: Are you trying to infer that any problem believers encounter do not come from the devil but from God. But at times through manifestation we hear the devil is the one causing the problem. What do you say about this?

ANS: The truth about this is that Christians cannot be possessed with demons nor can demons trouble them. We all know and accept the Holy Spirit lives in every Christian as a seal and guarantee of God's ownership. *"NOW IT IS GOD WHO MAKES BOTH US AND YOU STAND FIRM IN CHRIST. HE ANOINT US,* ***SET HIS SEAL OF OWNERSHIP ON US****, AND PUT HIS* ***SPIRIT*** *IN OUR* ***HEARTS*** *AS A DEPOSIT, GUARANTEEING WHAT IS TO COME".* 2Cor.1:21-22. (See Eph.1:13-14) If this is the case, then consider this question; how can the devil and the Holy Spirit live in the same body which is the temple of God? (See 1Cor.6:19) This tells us we have church goers—professed Christians among us, because the devil cannot harm nor live in the children of God. GOD CANNOT SHARE A ROOM WITH THE DEVIL!

According to the Bible passage we read from Isaiah 49:16, anyone who is a child of God has been ENGRAVED in the palm of Almighty God, so how come the devil is able to torment him? Those who are among us and able to be tormented by the devil, need to be converted properly. (See Acts 19:1-7. Also consider these texts for more enlightenments about this subject; 1John 5:18, Jer.20:11, Rom.8:31, Prov.1:33, Psalm 31:20)

2. **QUESTION:** The scriptures have explained clearly that we must all appear before the judgment seat of God, that each one may receive what is due to him for the things done while in the body, whether good or bad. (2Cor.5:10) Now what will happen if a woman or wife refuses to make her body available to her husband, and that results in adultery on the part of the husband, will that wife be judged for that?

ANS: The answer to this question is "YES", because women were created for men as a suitable mate (partner) because no suitable partner was found among the animals God created. After Women were created, God made a law that whoever has sexual relation with animals must be put to death. (See Exod.22:19)

Women were not in God's original plan in creation, but He realized man would find it difficult to survive without woman. *"The Lord God said it is not good for the man to live alone. I will make a helper suitable for him".* Gen.2:18. On the other hand, if it would have been good for a man to live alone, it means women would have not been created. Obviously, women were created for men because the man's way is with a woman. (See Prov.30:19). *"A MAN OUGHT NOT TO COVER HIS HEAD, SINCE HE IS THE IMAGE AND THE GLORY OF GOD: BUT THE WOMAN IS THE GLORY OF MAN. FOR MAN DID NOT COME FROM WOMAN, BUT WOMAN FROM MAN; NEITHER WAS MAN CREATED FOR WOMAN, BUT WOMAN FOR MAN".* 1Cor.11:7-9.

This passage reveals the reason women were created. God created man to take care of the earth, but He later realized as He needed man, man would also needed a partner—not just a partner but A SUITABLE PARTNER—WOMAN. In order to prove He was creating woman for the man, He took a part of man, and made woman out of it. Then He BROUGHT HER TO THE MAN, to indicate He created the woman for the man. (See Gen.2:18-23) That is why Apostle Paul confirmed that woman was created for man, and also woman was taken out of a man—so woman is for man! (1Cor.11:7-9) Now have you ever considered this question before? When God wanted the man to have a companion, why did He not create another man to be his assistant? I am trying to bring out a mystery of God's creation, but you must have the sound mind of God to receive this properly. With what the world has come to, it will be difficult for many to accept this mystery. (See 1Cor.2:10-16)

If you clearly understand the statement God made, you can see He realized Adam needed a SUITABLE HELPER, NOT JUST A HELPER! A helper who could help him in EVERYTHING—INCLUDING "SENSUAL PLEASURE" (See Gen.2:18, Eph.5:24). Another man could help the man to only a certain point in life, but a woman can help him in EVERYTHING. (See Prov.30:19, Prov.5:15-20, Eccl.9:9, Eccl.4:9-12, 1Peter 3:7)

In view of this, if any woman refuses or fails to fulfill the purpose in which she was created, and causes the man who was created in the image and the glory of God go out and commit adultery, she has failed to fulfill her duty for which her body was formed. Therefore, God will question her about it, because she has deprived her husband of her body causing him to consider receiving from another that which he should have received from her. However, God has made a provision for the woman. You may choose not to marry at all if you know you cannot deal the responsibilities in marriage and have the discipline to live without sexual intimacy. (See 1Cor.7:28-40) But if you want to marry, then consider this passage below.

"A WOMAN IS BOUND TO HER HUSBAND AS LONG AS HE LIVES". 1Cor.1:39.

3. **QUESTION:** You made a point that God hates divorce and quoted Malachi 2:16. So if anyone enters into marriage, it becomes imperative to stay in it till death separates you from your spouse. But the Bible makes it clear if your spouse commits adultery you can divorce her for that. (Matt.5:31-32). What do you say about this? Can marriage be broken in this way or cannot be broken at all?

ANS: Jesus Christ Himself answered this question clearly to you in Matthew 19:1-11. Some Pharisees came to test Him with this very question of yours. They asked Him; "*Is it lawful for a man to divorce his wife FOR ANY AND EVERY REASON? 'Haven't you read', he replied, that at the beginning the Creator made them male and female, and said (the rule in it) For this reason a man will **LEAVE** his father and mother and **BE UNITED** to his wife and the TWO will become **ONE FLESH**! So they are no longer two but ONE. **THEREFORE WHAT GOD HAS JOINED TOGETHER, LET MAN NOT SEPARATE.** Why then, they asked, did Moses command that a man give his wife a certificate of divorce and send her away? Jesus replied; Moses permitted you to divorce your **wife BECAUSE YOUR HEARTS WERE***

HARD. BUT IT WAS NOT THIS WAY FROM THE BEGINNING. *I tell you that anyone who divorce his wife, except for marital unfaithfulness and marries another woman commits adultery. The disciples said to him, if this is the situation between a wife and husband, it is* ***BETTER NOT TO MARRY.*** *Jesus replied; Not everyone can ACCEPT THIS WORD, but only those to whom it has been given".* Matt.19:1-11.

This is the answer to your question which was clearly explained by Jesus Himself. When He finished this explanation, His disciples were afraid to enter into marriage and later find themselves in A NO-TURNING BACK RELATIONSHIP. They said; "*If this is the situation between a husband and a wife, it is better not to marry".* Matt.19:10.

Are you also afraid of marriage? Take it easy, because marriage is not bad as you think. It's good, pleasant and enjoyable. How you begin the journey would determine how it ends. It begins with how you chose your spouse. Are you sure you sought God's counsel and guidance when you were choosing your spouse? If yes, then, why do you ask and bother yourself with this question? Those who relied on the Omniscient God to choose their spouses and continue to rely on Him really enjoy a good and peaceful marriage without bothering with this question and the answer thereof. But if you need more points on this question, then this passage will help you find a solution to your problem. "*TO THE MARRIED, I GIVE THIS COMMAND; (NOT I, BUT THE LORD)* ***A WIFE MUST NOT SEPARATE FROM HER HUSBAND****. BUT IF SHE DOES, SHE MUST REMAIN UNMARRIED OR ELSE BE RECONCILED TO HER HUSBAND.* ***AND THE HUSBAND MUST NOT DIVORCE HIS WIFE****".* 1Cor.7:10-11.

This passage summarizes the answer to your question—for God doesn't complicate His word!

4. **QUESTION: You made it clear that whatever happens to believers is allowed by God. I want to know how God deals with His erring children—believers. Does He give us to the devil just as He gave Job to him?**

ANS: Point for correction please; Job was not an erring believer. He was an upright and blameless man who feared God (See Job 1:8). Fortunately or unfortunately, God wanted to proof Satan wrong concerning his claim and charge against Job. This caused that innocent man so much trouble. (See Job 1:1-22, 2:1-13).

Now let's go on to your question: does the devil has a hand in God's discipline of His children? God has His own DESTROYING ANGELS who are sent out to cause havoc and agony to His erring children. "AND DO NOT GRUMBLE, AS SOME OF THEM DID—AND WERE KILLED BY THE DESTROYING ANGELS". 1Cor.10:10. (Also see 2 Sam. 24:15-17, 1 Sam. 18:10-12, 2 Chronicles 18:1-34.) "*WHY SHOULD THE LORD BE ANGRY WITH YOU AND DESTROY THE WORK OF YOUR HANDS?*" Eccl. 5:6.

All these passages show us Satan and his accomplices have no part to play when it comes to discipline. Nobody can discipline somebody's children except the parent alone. This discipline of God is being done by God's own destroying angels. He has some angels who protect believers and He has those He sent for service and the DESTROYING ONES.

These are some of the questions which were asked by some believers and I hope their answers may help you too, should in case some of these questions also bother or confuse you.

My dear readers, my aim for writing this book is not to portray God in a bad manner, or to cause fear in believers about God, but the Lord wants me to help believers to be CAUTIOUS OF SIN BUT NOT FEAR THE DEVIL. As Apostle Paul said, nothing on this earth or in heaven can separate us from the love of God which is in Christ Jesus. (See Rom.8:35-39) But Only SIN CAN SEPARATE a believer from God. (See Gen.3:1-24, Psalm 18:20-30, 145:17-20, Isaiah 63:10, Jer.30:11-15) Take some time to read these passages for more enlightenment.

CHAPTER 17

CONCLUSION

"We know that anyone born of God does not continue to sin; the one who was born of God KEEPS HIM SAFE, AND THE EVIL ONE CANNOT HARM HIM. We know that we are children of God, and ***the whole world is UNDER THE CONTROL OF THE EVIL ONE****. We know also that the Son of God has and has given us* ***UNDERSTANDING****; so that we may know him who is true. And we are in Him who is true—even in His Son Jesus Christ. He is the true God and eternal life.* ***DEAR CHILDREN, KEEP YOURSELVES FROM IDOLS (SINS)****"* 1 John 5:18-21.

This passage shows if anyone believes and accepts Jesus Christ and is born again, Satan and his accomplices have no power over him, and Satan is no more to be feared. This is the understanding He has given us, because God who is now his Father and redeemer is STRONG AND THE LORD ALMIGHTY is His name (See Jer.50:34, 20:11, Psalm 31:20). At this juncture, the devil does not just give up on him. He will try all that he can to fight over him hoping to win him back into his dominion. As is found in this book, the method or weapon he uses to wage war against us to subdue us is to entice, lure or cause us to rebel against our Father and redeemer. The devil has given his accomplices duty to make sure believers keep on doing what God HATES—anything which displeases and provokes Him is what they are causing believers to keep doing. So it is no wonder that believers continually break up their marriages routinely and rebel against God. (See Prov.4:16, Mal.2:16, Isaiah 63:10, 2Cor.2:11, 1 Peter 5:8)

Since the time set to destroy the devil and his accomplices have not come, they are still ruling the world. So if anyone refuses to accept Jesus Christ as Lord and personal Savior, the devil is able to torment him with whatever problems which please him (See Matt.8:29, John 14:30, 1 John 5:18-20). Therefore, if you are reading this book and you have not accepted Jesus Christ, you have the chance to accept Him now as your Lord and Personal Savior, and if you have accepted Him already, then KEEP YOURSELF FROM IDOLS AND EVIL THINGS! (See 1 John 5:21, 1 Peter 3:10-13)

Briefly, a born again believers should not acknowledge Satan in their problems and tribulations, because he has no right or power to torment them unless it is allowed by God. Therefore, believers should deal with God concerning their problems and predicaments. Ask God to give a command to keep you safe, and it will be done! I mean you must pray to God concerning your problems, and don't always set your eyes on Satan and pray against him, because he can only do what is permitted by God and you and your prayer cannot stop him of what is allowed or given to him to do. Of course you cannot stop him! (See Psalm 71:3, 71:1-24, Isaiah 54:16)

If you are encountering any problem and anyone tells you the devil has done that thing to you, DO NOT ACCEPT IT! If any pastor, prophet or any other person tells you your womb has been taken away from you by the devil and if you believe and know you are a child of God, please DO NOT ACCEPT IT! If you are encountering marital problems and anyone who claims to be a man of God, tells you it is the devil doing that, and you know you are a child of God, please DO NOT ACCEPT IT! In fact, no-one who believes and knows he is a child of Almighty God will admit Satan is in-charge of his problems. If Satan has the right and a chance to worry us, then, he would have killed us long time, because we are his greatest enemy. Fortunately, we are not dealing with him but with our heavenly Father, and this gives us hope that we will not be put to SHAME! (See Jer.29:11, Rom.10:11)

In this book, the two words I have used mainly for the true children of God are BELIEVERS AND CHRISTIANS. We know that everyone who attends church service and have registered their names to be called Christians and believers. I say this in order for you to not be confused of the way I addressed and explained some of these subjects. When I mention "believer" or "Christian," of which I advice to not bother themselves with the devil, I refer to those who worship the Father in Spirit and truth. (John 4:23-24)

There are some people who PROFESS to serve the Lord, and yet rely on their own efforts to obey His law, to form a right character and to secure salvation. Their hearts are not moved by the love of God, and their hearts are not controlled by the Holy Spirit. They seek to perform the duties of a Christian as if that is what God requires of them in order to get to heaven. Such religion is worth nothing. Satan and his accomplices can still control them to disgrace the name of the Lord and can torment them with whatever problems which please them. These people worship God in VAIN! (See Mark 7:6-9)

Again, there are some people who have been misled by the agents of Satan masqueraded as men of God. All of them are also known as believers or Christians, though they are really not because they live in a lie. For that matter, the devil and his accomplices can still control and torment them however they want. (See Rev.2:9, 2Thess.2:9-12). *"FOR SUCH PERSONS ARE FALSE APOSTLES, DECEITFUL WORKERS, MASQUERADING AS APOSTLES OF CHRIST. AND NO WONDER, FOR SATAN HIMSELF MASQUERADES AS AN ANGEL OF LIGHT. IT IS NOT SURPRISING, THEN, IF HIS SERVANTS ALSO MASQUERADE AS SERVANTS OF RIGHTEOUSNESS. THEIR END WILL BE WHAT THEIR ACTIONS DESERVE"*. 2Cor.11:13-15. If anyone is worshipping God with these people, he cannot claim the benefits and the privileges I'm talking about in this book, unless he repents and converts in the proper way and place. (John 4:23-24, 2Tim.2:22)

The Christians and believers I am talking about in this book are those who have given their lives fully to Christ in the right place and are holding on to His teachings. (See John 14:15, Luke 6:46-49, 1 John 3:9-11, 3:16-24) A Christian is the one who is been controlled or led by the Spirit of God. (Rom.8:14)

When a Christian is being led by the Spirit of God, the heart becomes filled with His love, the joy of communion with Him and cleaves to Him; and with the contemplation of Him; selfish desire is forgotten. The love of Christ then becomes the spring of his action. This is the believer to whom

I'm talking in this book; and the devil has no power to afflict him with anything unless God Himself allows him. Those who feel the constraining love of God do not ask how they may meet the requirements of God; they do not set standards, but aim at the perfect conformity to the will of God. With earnest desire, they yield and manifest an interest proportional to the value of the object which they seek. Life in Christ without this love is mere talk, dry formality and heavy drudgery, because the kingdom of God is not a matter of TALK BUT OF POWER AND COMPLETE OBEDIENT TO GOD! (See 1Cor.4:20, 2Cor.10:3-6)

"NOW TO HIM WHO IS ABLE TO ESTABLISH YOU BY MY GOSPEL (in this book) AND THE PROCLAMATION OF JESUS CHRIST, ACCORDING TO THE REVELATION OF THE MYSTERY HIDDEN FOR LONG PAST, BUT NOW REVEALED AND MADE KNOWN THROUGH THE PROPHETIC WRITING (of this book) BY THE COMMAND OF THE ETERNAL GOD SO THAT ALL NATIONS MIGHT BELIEVE AND OBEY HIM TO THE ONLY TRUE AND WISE GOD BE THE GLORY FOR EVER THROUGH JESUS CHRIST— **AMEN!"** (Rom.16:25-27)

Printed in the United States
by Baker & Taylor Publisher Services